Hazelden Co-occurring Disorders Program

Integrated Services for Substance Use and Mental Health Problems

Cognitive-Behavioral Therapy for People with Co-occurring Disorders

Mark McGovern, Ph.D.
and other faculty from the Geisel School of Medicine at Dartmouth

HAZELDEN®

Hazelden
Center City, Minnesota 55012
hazelden.org

ISBN: 978-1-61649-544-2

Editor's note

The names, details, and circumstances may have been changed to protect the privacy
of those mentioned in this publication.

This publication is not intended as a substitute for the advice of health care
professionals.

Alcoholics Anonymous and AA are registered trademarks of Alcoholics Anonymous
World Services, Inc.

The terms *mental health disorder, mental health problem,* and *psychiatric disorder*
are all used interchangeably throughout the Co-occurring Disorders Program. These
three terms refer to a non-severe diagnosis. The selection of terms used in each
component of the program may reflect the preference of the individual author.

Cover and interior design by Kinne Design
Typesetting by Kinne Design and Madeline Berglund
Illustrations by Patrice Barton

ABOUT THE AUTHORS

Mark McGovern

Mark McGovern, Ph.D., is a Professor of Psychiatry and of Community and Family Medicine at the Geisel School of Medicine at Dartmouth in Lebanon, New Hampshire. He practices at the Dartmouth Hitchcock Medical Center, and his research program is based at the Dartmouth Psychiatric Research Center. His clinical and research focus is integrated treatment for persons with co-occurring substance use and psychiatric disorders. Dr. McGovern has received a NIDA career development award and federal research grant funding to translate evidence-based therapies for co-occurring disorders into routine clinical settings. He has also received awards from the Robert Wood Johnson Foundation and the Substance Abuse and Mental Health Services Administration to advance a series of organizational measures of integrated service capacity. These measures, the Dual Diagnosis Capability in Addiction Treatment (DDCAT), Dual Diagnosis Capability in Mental Health Treatment (DDCMHT) and Dual Diagnosis Capability in Health Care Settings (DDCHCS), have been widely adopted and are being used to implement evidence-based treatments in community settings throughout the United States. Dr. McGovern has been actively involved in the education of medical students, psychiatric residents and fellows, and clinical psychology interns at Dartmouth and previously at Northwestern University Medical School in Chicago. Since 2009, he has been the editor-in-chief for the *Journal of Substance Abuse Treatment*, the leading scientific journal dedicated to addiction treatment research and implementation.

Robert E. Drake

Robert E. Drake, M.D., Ph.D., is the Andrew Thomson Professor of Psychiatry and of Community and Family Medicine at the Geisel School of Medicine at Dartmouth and the director of the Dartmouth Psychiatric Research Center. He has been at Dartmouth since 1984 and is currently vice chair and director of research in the Department of Psychiatry. He works as a community mental health doctor and researcher. His research focuses on co-occurring disorders, vocational rehabilitation, health services research, and evidence-based practices. He has written more than twenty books and more than 500 papers about co-occurring disorders, vocational rehabilitation, mental health services, evidence-based practices, and shared decision making.

Matthew R. Merrens

Matthew R. Merrens, Ph. D., has served as codirector of the Dartmouth Evidence-Based Practices Center and as visiting professor of psychiatry at Dartmouth Medical School. He received his Ph.D. in clinical psychology at the University of Montana and was formerly on the faculty and the chair of the Psychology Department at the State University of

New York at Plattsburgh. He has extensive experience in clinical psychology and community mental health and has authored and edited textbooks on the psychology of personality, introductory psychology, the psychology of development, and social psychology. He recently published a book on evidence-based mental health practices and has also served as director of the Dartmouth Summer Institute in Evidence-Based Psychiatry and Mental Health.

Kim T. Mueser

Kim T. Mueser, Ph.D., is a clinical psychologist, executive director of the Center for Psychiatric Rehabilitation, and professor in the Departments of Occupational Therapy, Psychiatry, and Psychology at Boston University. Dr. Mueser's clinical and research interests include the treatment of co-occurring psychiatric and substance use disorders, family psychoeducation, psychiatric rehabilitation for serious mental illnesses, and the treatment of posttraumatic stress disorder. His research has been supported by the National Institute of Mental Health, the National Institute on Drug Abuse, the Substance Abuse and Mental Health Administration, and the National Alliance for Research on Schizophrenia and Depression. He is the co-author of more than ten books and treatment manuals and has published numerous articles in peer-reviewed journals. Dr. Mueser has also given numerous lectures and workshops on the treatment of co-occurring disorders and psychiatric rehabilitation, both nationally and internationally.

Mary F. Brunette

Mary F. Brunette, M.D., is an Associate Professor of Psychiatry at the Geisel School of Medicine at Dartmouth. She has been working in the field of treatment for patients with co-occurring disorders for twenty years. She conducts research on services and medications for people with co-occurring substance use and serious mental illness. She is a clinician who provides treatment for patients with co-occurring disorders. She also is medical director of the Bureau of Behavioral Health in the New Hampshire Department of Health and Human Services. She has published more than fifty articles and book chapters, many related to medication treatment for people with co-occurring disorders. She speaks nationally on this topic.

. . .

Hazelden Co-occurring Disorders Program

Integrated Services for Substance Use and Mental Health Problems

PROGRAM COMPONENTS

The Co-occurring Disorders Program is made up of a guidebook, five curricula, and a DVD. These components can stand alone, but when used together they provide a comprehensive, evidence-based program for the treatment of persons with co-occurring substance use and psychiatric disorders.

← ***A Leader's Guide to Implementing Integrated Services***
Includes a guidebook and a CD-ROM.

Screening and Assessment →
Includes a clinician's guide and a CD-ROM.

← ***Integrating Combined Therapies: Motivational Enhancement Therapy, Cognitive-Behavioral Therapy, and Twelve Step Facilitation***
Includes a clinician's guide and a CD-ROM.

Cognitive-Behavioral Therapy →
Includes a clinician's guide and a CD-ROM.

← ***Medication Management***
Includes a clinician's guide and a CD-ROM.

Family Program: Education, Skills, and Therapy →
Includes a clinician's guide and a CD-ROM.

← ***A Guide for Living with Co-occurring Disorders: Help and Hope for Clients and Their Families***
Ninety-minute DVD.

CONTENTS

▼

ACKNOWLEDGMENTS

The material in this guide draws heavily from three primary sources: (1) K. T. Mueser, M. K. Jankowski, J. L. Hamblen, S. D. Rosenberg, M. Descamps, M. P. Salyers, and E. E. Bolton, *Cognitive Behavioral Therapy for PTSD in People with Severe Mental Illness: Therapist Manual* (Concord, NH: Dartmouth Psychiatric Research Center, 2004); (2) M. P. McGovern, *Cognitive Behavioral Therapy for PTSD in Addiction Treatment Programs: Therapist Manual*, version 3.0 (Lebanon, NH: Dartmouth Psychiatric Research Center, 2007), available at dms.dartmouth.edu/prc/dual/atsr/; and (3) *Cognitive Behavioral Therapy for PTSD in Addiction Treatment Programs: Client Workbook*, version 3.0 (Lebanon, NH: Dartmouth Psychiatric Research Center, 2007), available at dms.dartmouth.edu/prc/dual/atsr/. The results of the applications of these treatments are also described in M. P. McGovern, A. I. Alterman, K. M. Drake, and A. P. Dauten, "Co-occurring PTSD and Substance Use Disorders in Addiction Treatment Settings," in *Treating Posttraumatic Stress Disorders in Special Populations*, ed. K. T. Mueser and S. Rosenberg (Washington, DC: American Psychological Association Press, 2008).

The authors would like to acknowledge the clinicians and patients who provided feedback on their experience using earlier versions of this guide. In particular, we would like to thank the clinicians who participated in developmental studies with CBT for co-occurring disorders in addiction treatment programs: Lois Hollow, Karen Gillock, Ellen Eberhart, Melissa Edney, and Jim Gamache. We are also grateful to the leadership of six addiction treatment agencies who are actively involved in the development and research of the guides, in particular, Phil Richmond, Aliza Castro, and Jim Moutinho of the Hartford Dispensary (Hartford and New Britain, Connecticut); Bruce Hart of Retreat Healthcare (Brattleboro, Vermont); Renee Thayer of the Clara Martin Center (Wilder, Vermont); Lisa Houle of Farnum Rehabilitation Program (Manchester, New Hampshire); Catherine Ulrich of the Dartmouth-Hitchcock Medical Center Addiction Treatment Program (Hanover, New Hampshire); and Tim Hartnett of Comprehensive Options for Drug Abuse, Inc. (Portland, Oregon).

Without the efforts and passion on the part of those on the "front lines," this work would be neither possible nor relevant.

• • •

▼

How to Build a Patient Workbook

The patient workbook is a critical component for providing structure within the Co-occurring Disorders Program. Without it, treatment and management of the educational materials, handouts, and worksheets for the patients can become disorganized and thus less effective. People in recovery with co-occurring disorders need structure. Organization is crucial in achieving coherence and usefulness of these patient materials. In order to effectively implement the Co-occurring Disorders Program, you will need to do the following:

- **Print** the reproducible handouts from the sessions or modules in each curriculum. (A CD-ROM containing PDFs of these reproducible pages is packaged with each curriculum.) Make extra copies of the handouts to have on hand during sessions, especially when using the curricula *Integrating Combined Therapies, Cognitive-Behavioral Therapy,* and *Family Program.*

- **Compile** the handouts in a three-ring binder or a folder for each patient.

- **Customize** your patients' workbooks by using the sample cover (found on the CD-ROM) of each of the three curricula mentioned above.

- **Give** each patient a workbook upon admission to your program.

- **Decide** whether the workbook will be kept by the clinician at your center/clinic or taken home with the patient. This decision can be jointly made with the patient.

- **Include** extra handouts whenever necessary.

· · ·

Part I

INTRODUCTION

This curriculum describes a cognitive-behavioral therapy (CBT) approach for persons with co-occurring substance use and psychiatric disorders. This CBT curriculum is primarily designed for delivery in the context of an addiction treatment program. The addiction treatment program may be drug free, abstinence based, methadone maintenance, or medication-assisted recovery based. It is important to understand that co-occurring disorders require intensive and adequate treatment for the substance use disorder. Integrated or augmented psychiatric or psychosocial treatments may only be effective under such conditions (i.e., the patient is receiving treatment for his or her substance use disorder at the same time he or she is involved in CBT).

For the sake of convenience, the word "clinician" refers to any practitioner—counselors, supervisors, therapists, psychologists, facilitators, medical and mental health personnel, administrators, agency directors, and doctors—using this guide and curriculum as part of the Co-occurring Disorders Program with patients and family members.

This curriculum may also be used in office-based or mental health programs either alone or in tandem with other services. It is important to ascertain the severity of the substance use problem to determine if this CBT treatment can be effective under these circumstances. For example, in the context of active substance use, it may be clinically necessary for the patient to be placed in a more intense level of care to stabilize the substance use problem. If, however, the patient is stable, or in a period of early or advanced recovery, then this treatment may be delivered within the context of an office-based or mental health practice.

It is important to understand that co-occurring disorders require intensive and adequate treatment for the substance use disorder.

The treatment outlined in this guide consists of several important clinical practices:

1. Asking about substance use: You must ask patients about substance use initially and throughout the course of the treatment. Patients with co-occurring disorders are at high risk for relapse to substance use. Multiple factors will make it challenging for them to sustain abstinence or to discontinue the use of substances as a primary coping strategy to manage psychiatric symptoms.

2. Asking about psychiatric symptoms: You must ask patients about psychiatric symptoms initially and throughout the course of treatment. Patients may be relying less on substances to cope with their psychiatric symptoms, such as anxiety and depression, or have more severe symptoms related to PTSD. As a result, they will be in a position to learn new coping skills. In the meantime, until they develop new coping skills through CBT, they may feel at a temporary loss for how to manage their psychiatric symptoms.

3. Establishing safety: At the first session, you must talk about issues of substance use, ongoing or acute psychiatric symptoms, and risk for self-harm, including suicide. It is important to determine if a patient is safe and stable enough to participate in the treatment. Developing a relapse prevention and crisis plan in the first session will permit an open discussion of these issues and delineate appropriate courses of action.

4. Teaching breathing retraining: Teach breathing retraining early on as a way for patients to immediately begin to manage their anxiety, and have patients practice breathing retraining throughout their treatment. Anxiety is one of the most common symptoms across all psychiatric disorders, and having a skill to manage it is important.

5. Educating patients: Using the Fact Sheet for each major psychiatric disorder (including a general one on co-occurring disorders) as a guide, you will provide patients with basic information about their disorders and related problems. These same Fact Sheets will also be used in other components of the Co-occurring Disorders Program: *Integrating Combined Therapies* and *Family Program*. Patients will also be given additional handouts in each module. For additional patient information on specific disorders, see the CD-ROM for a list of other Hazelden products.

6. Teaching cognitive restructuring (CR): You will be teaching patients how to challenge automatic thoughts that lead to upsetting feelings. CR is a core ingredient of CBT.

7. Generalization and beyond: Since CBT is a time-limited, skill-based therapy, you will need to prepare the patient for the end of treatment (termination) in advance. Explain that with time and practice he or she will continue to develop the ability to use CR even after the treatment has ended. Through this process, he or she will become his or her own clinician.

8. Discussing follow-ups to CBT: You will need to discuss with patients what types of services they will continue to receive in the addiction treatment or mental health program. Since addiction and psychiatric disorders are typically chronic and involve a vulnerability to relapse, patients will need to consider ongoing monitoring of both problems for the foreseeable future.

• • •

You will need to discuss with patients what types of services they will continue to receive in the addiction treatment or mental health program.

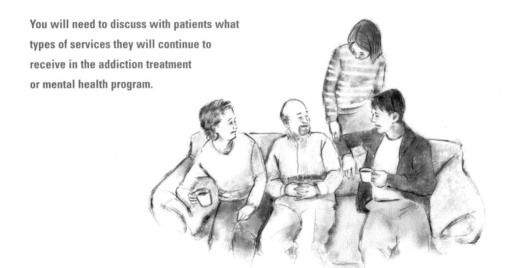

Core Principles of Cognitive-Behavioral Therapy

Although many versions of CBT exist, several principles cut across all forms to make it a more "generic" type of psychological therapy. With some variation for application to specific disorders, most CBT shares the same common ingredients. This version of CBT focuses on cognitive restructuring. Other versions of CBT may focus on behaviors, such as in imaginal or in vivo exposure to anxiety-producing situations. Yet others may focus on the development of alternative coping skills. Although the versions of CBT may lean in several different directions, they all share common principles. The execution of these basic principles makes it recognizable as CBT and distinct from other therapies. The following information describes those shared principles.

CBT Is Present Centered

CBT differs from many other psychological therapies in that its focus is on the present or "here-and-now." It does not dwell on the long or distant causes of a problem, but instead focuses on what is happening now.

CBT Focuses on Thoughts and Their Interpretation That Give Rise to Negative or Positive Feelings

CBT also does not so much focus on the patient's feelings, as much as it focuses on the thoughts that give rise to the feelings. In fact, CBT is based on the assumption that a cascade of negative thoughts leads to irrational fears, worries, hopelessness, worthlessness, avoidance, and many other negative feelings and behaviors. CBT will also help a person understand which kinds of thoughts lead to positive feelings such as hope, joy, excitement, empathy, and inspiration.

CBT Focuses on Learning New Ways of Thinking

The therapy is then focused on helping the patient examine the sequence of events from situations to thoughts to feelings and understand that there is more flexibility in altering thoughts than the patient may have ever imagined. The CBT clinician wedges the possibility of new ways of thinking in response to previously set interpretations about situations, events, or beliefs. This tactical skill is taught to the patient in the context of the therapy so that the patient learns to apply this technique on his or her own. For this guide, this technique is called "cognitive restructuring" (CR).

CBT Involves Identifying Common Styles of Thinking

During the course of examining their ways of thinking about potentially negative situations, and how these ways of thinking lead to negative thoughts and feelings, patients will learn to recognize common thinking errors or cognitive distortions. Sometimes these distortions are less judgmentally called "common styles of thinking." For example, one common thinking style among people with depression or anxiety disorders is "catastrophic thinking." Catastrophic thinking, or catastrophizing, typically involves predicting the worst case scenario without evidence. Thus, a person with social anxiety may avoid group situations because he fears the worst will happen: that he will become anxious or embarrassed; he will be unable to control it; everyone will notice it; and, finally, he will be even more humiliated. Given this prediction of certainty, it is no wonder he avoids these kinds of situations.

CBT Is Skill Based

Learning new ways to process situations and thoughts so that new feelings and behaviors can emerge is a skill. CBT is focused on the clinician teaching the patient how to use this skill and how to apply it to key aspects of his or her life.

CBT Involves Practice

Acquiring any new skill is a combination of learning it correctly and then applying it over and over. Once a patient learns the technique of CR, he or she benefits by repetition in his or her life. The more a patient practices this skill in real-world situations, the better he or she will get at it. In fact, most successful outcomes for CBT occur when patients complete their practice exercises between sessions. These exercises enable the patient to replace formerly automatic thoughts that

Learning new ways to process situations and thoughts so that new feelings and behaviors can emerge is a skill.

led to negative feelings (such as anxiety or depression) with reflexive thoughts that are more flexible and positive.

CBT Requires Clinician Activity

The CBT clinician in many ways is a teacher or coach. Certain skills are first presented and explained. The patient demonstrates the skill in the session. This sequence is repeated several times with different examples. The patient is assigned practice (homework) between sessions. This material is carefully reviewed at the start of each new session. Clinicians are not passive and are more instructional. At the same time, the CBT clinician is tuned into the patient's needs, comfort, and learning styles. The clinician adjusts the pace, the timing, and, to some extent, the approach to maximize the patient's chances for success.

CBT Is Time Limited

CBT is time limited. The goal of the clinician is to make sure the patient can serve as his or her own clinician by learning and internalizing the skills of CR so thoroughly that the clinician is no longer needed. The time-limited nature of CBT is underscored several times at the outset of the therapy, and the patient is reminded throughout the course of the treatment. Many patients, particularly those having experience with other therapies, initially find this difficult to accept. Often these very same patients learn in time to appreciate the autonomy of CBT. They become proud of their capacity to do the techniques on their own.

Follow-up or booster sessions are not uncommon, so they may be incorporated into the generalization phase of CBT. CBT could also be built into "recovery checkups" that may occur for patients in maintenance or relapse prevention stages. For more information about recovery checkups, see module 20 in the curriculum *Integrating Combined Therapies*.

Summary

Although there are different manifestations or applications of CBT, most share common principles and ingredients. It is important for the CBT clinician to be familiar with these principles. Clinicians new to CBT may need to consider how these principles are similar to or different from their typical therapeutic strategies and assumptions. A skilled CBT clinician will also answer patients' questions about how CBT works and how it may differ from their own previous therapy experiences.

• • •

Duplicating this page is illegal. Do not copy this material without written permission from the publisher.

9

The Effectiveness of CBT for Co-occurring Substance Use and Psychiatric Disorders

CBT is a well-established evidence-based practice for both substance use and psychiatric disorders. It has been found effective with a heterogeneous group of disorders and therefore might be considered a generic practice that can be helpful with any mental health or behavioral problem.

The sections below briefly review the evidence for the effectiveness of CBT as applied to both substance use and psychiatric disorders, as well as for co-occurring disorders.

CBT and Substance Use Disorders

In the largest multisite trials ever conducted by the National Institute on Alcohol Abuse and Alcoholism (NIAAA) and the National Institute on Drug Abuse (NIDA), CBT was the only intervention researched for both agencies. In the NIAAA Project MATCH studies, CBT was compared to motivational enhancement therapy (MET) and Twelve Step facilitation (TSF) therapy and was found equally effective. (Note that the combination of these treatment approaches fits into a stage-wise treatment model and is adapted for persons with co-occurring disorders in the curriculum *Integrating Combined Therapies.*) In the NIDA multisite Collaborative Cocaine Treatment Study, cognitive therapy (CT) was compared to three other manual-guided treatments: supportive-expressive psychotherapy (SEP), individual drug counseling (IDC), and group drug counseling (GDC). Both IDC and GDC were designed to be "treatments-as-usual" but performed at least as well as the CT and SEP approaches.

The manuals used in the NIAAA and NIDA studies shared many of the common ingredients outlined in chapter 1 of this guide. A number of studies both before these multisite trials and since have replicated the effectiveness of CBT in reducing substance use and enhancing recovery.

Relapse prevention therapy (RPT) is also a well-established evidence-based practice for substance use disorders. RPT is by its core principles a type of CBT. RPT focuses on the antecedents and consequences of behaviors. It helps a patient recognize sequences of seemingly irrelevant events and develop alternative coping skills. Like CBT, RPT involves a clinician that is akin to a teacher or coach. He or she encourages the patient to develop improved self-monitoring skills via practice between sessions.

CBT is also one of the most desired approaches among community clinicians in terms of training and implementation.

CBT and Psychiatric Disorders

Although CBT roots date back to behavior therapy and systematic desensitization, most consider the origins of CBT to have started with the work of Aaron Beck. Beck initially studied CBT for depression and found it to be as effective as medications. Since then, CBT has been studied and found effective for mood disorders as well as anxiety disorders.

Derivations of CBT have been used to help persons with schizophrenia and bipolar disorder develop new skills and improved capability to manage their illnesses. Adaptations of CBT have also been used for persons with personality disorders, specifically borderline personality disorder (with dialectical behavioral therapy). Recent studies have used single generic manuals for CBT for a heterogeneous group of psychiatric disorders and found it effective.

For psychiatric disorders, CBT is perhaps the most effective psychosocial intervention. In combination with the FDA-approved medications for the psychiatric disorder, concomitant CBT is the treatment of choice. In the case of some disorders, such as PTSD and social anxiety disorder, CBT has been found more effective than medication, both in terms of the magnitude of patient change and also the durability of change over time.

For psychiatric disorders, CBT is perhaps the most effective psychosocial intervention.

CBT for Co-occurring Substance Use and Psychiatric Disorders

In both NIDA- and NIAAA-funded research, versions of CBT have been applied to persons with anxiety disorders (such as panic disorder and social anxiety disorder) and alcohol use disorder, and persons with PTSD and cocaine use disorder. These studies, although limited by rather restrictive patient-inclusion criteria, converge in finding that CBT is effective for the symptoms of both substance use and psychiatric disorders. Two recent studies—one on people with bipolar disorder and the other on people with PTSD—have also found that CBT is promising in its effectiveness for patients in community addiction treatment programs who have a variety of substance and polysubstance use disorders.

Summary

Taken together, these studies suggest that the core principles of CBT for co-occurring substance use and psychiatric disorders have a strong evidence base.

• • •

CHAPTER 3

Translating CBT for Co-occurring Disorders into Routine Clinical Practice

Although CBT has widespread and generic effectiveness for many disorders, it is not readily available in routine clinical practice settings. Some have argued that this may be because CBT requires purposeful effort on the part of the clinician, rather than a more passive approach. Others have noted that CBT may be difficult to learn and even more difficult to deliver with adherence and competence.

Another reason may be that many of the manuals for CBT are very specific for particular disorders (for example, depression, anxiety disorders, PTSD, or bipolar disorder). However, most practitioners do not see patients with one particular psychiatric or substance use disorder. In fact, a more complex and heterogeneous patient profile is likely the rule. Patients often have problems with multiple substances, including alcohol *and* drugs or more than one drug. Further, patients may have more than one psychiatric disorder and certainly not all patients will present with the same disorder. Thus, a generic CBT manual that could address a range of psychiatric and substance use disorders, while still using the core principles, is needed.

This curriculum is intended to be a practical, ready-to-use CBT guide (with patient handouts) that can be used in routine clinical practice with a broad range of persons who suffer from co-occurring substance use and psychiatric disorders.

Patients often have problems with multiple substances, including alcohol *and* drugs or more than one drug.

This guide is an adaptation of *Cognitive Behavioral Therapy for PTSD in People with Severe Mental Illness: Therapist Manual*, which was itself adapted and simplified for persons with PTSD and co-occurring substance use disorders treated in community addiction treatment programs. These community addiction treatment programs range from intensive outpatient drug-free ones to methadone maintenance clinics in urban and rural settings. This CBT guide was developed for use by addiction and mental health clinicians who have limited training and expertise in CBT. Thus, it is designed to be simple and easy to use.

Researchers who study implementation effectiveness of evidence-based treatment have found several good predictors of a treatment's success in routine clinical practice. They include the following:

- The practice is simple to do and easy to learn.
- Clinicians are motivated to learn and do it.
- Clinicians see that their patients get better.
- The agency within which the practice is being delivered values it, and there is supervisory support for it.
- There are financial incentives to support it, or at least no financial factors to undermine it.

This guide should meet the first three criteria. We expect this guide to appeal to clinicians for its simplicity and ease of use. In addition, clinicians will likely be motivated to learn CBT and can expect to see their patients improve as a result of their efforts in CR. The fourth and fifth criteria are beyond the scope of our control.

Summary

This curriculum is meant to be a practical, ready-to-use CBT guide that can be used in routine clinical practice with a broad range of persons who suffer from co-occurring substance use and psychiatric disorders.

• • •

CHAPTER 4

Relationship Factors: Therapeutic Alliance and the Therapeutic Frame

Those who develop, study, and write about evidence-based practices acknowledge that it is essential for the delivery of the practice to occur within the context of a good relationship in order to be effective. Interestingly, some studies (such as the NIDA Collaborative Cocaine Treatment Study and NIAAA Project MATCH) that compared a group of evidence-based practices found that the therapeutic relationship accounts for considerable effects, sometimes above and beyond the properties of any specific intervention.

Taken to an extreme, some clinicians posit that effective therapy is all about the relationship between the clinician and patient. In the early days of psychotherapy research, scientist-practitioners such as Hans Strupp and others labeled this relationship a "nonspecific" factor, as if it could be considered somehow separate from the type of therapy being delivered or the specific technique being practiced. Other nonspecific factors included the positive safe and caring relationship, the expectation of change, the effect of time, homeostatic properties (a person starting out feeling bad will eventually return to a more baseline state), unconditional positive regard, and simply having a coherent explanation of the problem.

A less polemical interpretation of this issue suggests that both the type of practice and the relationship within which it occurs are critical to effective treatment. Most studies of practices, including CBT, have found the particular evidence-based treatment under study to be even more effective when compared with practices delivered by good clinicians with good relationships with patients. The effectiveness of CBT was above and beyond these treatments as usual.

This guide can only be effective to the degree to which the patient experiences the clinician as having his or her best interest in mind.

Nevertheless, this guide can only be effective to the degree to which the patient experiences the clinician as having his or her best interest in mind. In addition, the patient must sense that the clinician "understands" him or her, can communicate this understanding clearly and simply, and that they are working on common goals. Early measures of the therapeutic relationship focused precisely on these three factors: bond, rapport, and goals.

To these factors we add two specific ingredients to the therapeutic relationship that we would advise the CBT clinician to attend to: the therapeutic alliance and the therapeutic frame.

Therapeutic Alliance

The therapeutic alliance refers to the relationship between the clinician and patient that fosters an atmosphere conducive to achieving therapy goals. Clinicians should establish an emotionally contained yet active interchange with patients. If the patient is inhibited, the clinician attempts to engage him or her with open-ended questions. If the patient readily experiences feelings with associated increased emotional arousal, the clinician focuses on containment with supportive empathy, close-ended questions, and gentle redirection. Containment occurs, therefore, in not provoking more or deeper feelings, or in excavating for newer or more troubling ones. In order for the patient to progress toward therapy goals, the clinician must establish himself or herself as empathic and supportive yet task-focused. In addition, the clinician must establish the therapy as a place that is contained and safe. Clinicians should maintain this alliance with the patient throughout the treatment.

Therapeutic Frame

The term "therapeutic frame" was originally used by the psychoanalyst Robert Langs, and later elaborated on by interpersonal psychoanalysts Merton Gill and Irwin Hoffman. The frame refers to the structure and boundaries of the therapy within which the therapy and therapeutic relationship take place. Clinicians should manage the therapeutic frame of the session with the utmost awareness, diligence, and detail-mindedness. Patients with substance use disorders can be exquisitely sensitive to deviations in the therapeutic frame and can interpret deviations as a violation of trust.

Of particular importance is the clinician's ability to (1) start sessions punctually and hold them to a consistent duration, (2) provide sufficient notice for sessions he or she will have to cancel, (3) manage his or her own feelings, (4) clearly communicate what and when material is discussed with the addiction treatment program staff members who work with the patient, and, finally, (5) negotiate contacts between sessions. Consistency and reliability are essential aspects to managing the therapeutic frame.

To help clinicians understand how to work within the therapeutic frame, we have outlined three key dimensions that we visualize as a triangle (see figure 1). Competent therapy takes place within a field bounded by three margins or boundaries. Therapy outside of these relational or behavioral margins may be less effective. One margin represents a clinician who is rushed, haphazard, disorganized, or chaotic in conducting the session. Another margin represents a clinician who is overinvolved and hyperloquacious. This clinician may talk too much, cut the patient off, and in some cases use inappropriate self-disclosure. A third margin represents a clinician who is cold, distant, or pedagogical (preaching, lecturing).

A competent clinician works within the margins of this therapeutic triangle much like a tennis player strives to keep the ball within the white lines.

FIGURE 1

Therapeutic Triangle

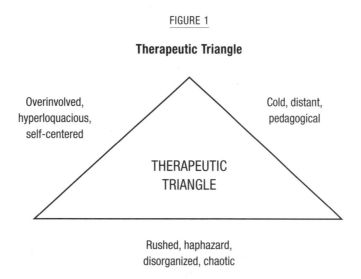

Summary

In order for CBT or any therapy for co-occurring disorders to be effective, a good therapeutic relationship is a prerequisite. Although there are many ways to understand key aspects to the therapeutic relationship, the therapeutic alliance and therapeutic frame are two that we recommend.

• • •

CHAPTER 5

How to Use This Guide

This curriculum is designed for direct application. You can use the text or provided scripts to guide the words you use with patients. In addition, use the formats in sequence or steps to progress through the treatment. Each module is formatted with instructional design for clarity and ease of use. Although this design may seem cookbook or boilerplate, how you conduct the therapy and deliver the material will be entirely up to you. Of course, if you deviate from the format and sequence to a large extent, and do things other than noted, the treatment you administer may not really be considered CBT for co-occurring disorders. For this reason, we have developed a Clinician (and Supervisor) Checklist to help you stay on track (located on the program CD-ROM and in the three-ring binder following the handouts). Each module in this curriculum concludes with this checklist.

Before you start to use this curriculum in your practice, first read about these five very important considerations:

- context: the setting where you work
- format: individual or group therapy
- session structure: length and purpose
- practice: a kinder word for homework
- plan and duration to deliver the curriculum

Each of these considerations is critically important. Be sure to read this section before starting to use this guide.

If the patient is not in addiction treatment and you are using this curriculum, you will need to more closely monitor the substance use.

1. Context

This curriculum is primarily organized to target a psychiatric disorder within the context of a substance use disorder. Therefore, this curriculum makes certain assumptions about the substance use disorder and its treatment. If you are using this curriculum in the context of an addiction treatment program (whether it is a residential, intensive outpatient, outpatient, drug-free, or medication-assisted program), you will find this curriculum comprehensive and ready to implement as is, because the patient is likely in an appropriate level of care to match the severity of the substance use disorder. Also, in addiction treatment, the patient is receiving educational sessions, learning new skills, and developing recovery supports for his or her addiction. This curriculum will fit in readily with services such as these. It will be easily integrated.

If you are a clinician in a mental health clinic or practice without additional services or recovery support programming for the patient's substance use disorder, you may find this curriculum does not focus as much on addiction as is needed. This will be true for patients who are unstable or in very early recovery from substance use disorders, but less so for those receiving parallel or concurrent treatment in an addiction treatment program, or who are in the maintenance or relapse prevention stage.

Nevertheless, if the patient is not in addiction treatment and you are using this curriculum, you will need to more closely monitor the substance use. (In addiction treatment programs, for instance, patients are often objectively monitored via urinalysis or Breathalyzer.) Also, you will need to be sure that the patient is in an appropriate level of care such that his or her active substance use is not placing him or her or others in danger. Lastly, you may need to augment this guide with material from the curriculum *Integrating Combined Therapies*. Office-based practitioners may use this curriculum in an integrated manner but should be quick to recognize if they need to incorporate the expertise of additional providers. Such practitioners should be aware that a patient may need stabilization in hospital (for acute psychiatric symptoms or medically managed detoxification services) or residential settings (to interrupt compulsive substance use or to provide a safe and supportive recovery environment).

If you are not familiar with how to determine the appropriate setting or level of care for persons with substance use disorders, you are advised to obtain the guidelines in *American Society of Addiction Medicine Patient Placement Criteria-3rd edition (ASAM PPC-3)*.

2. Format

Individual Sessions for Each Module

This guide is written for individual or one-on-one therapy. However, sessions can be easily used in group formats as well. (See the section entitled "Group Sessions.") For individual formats, you will be able to adjust the pace and focus of the session based on patient response. Unfortunately, if the patient is seen individually, he or she will not have as much opportunity for vicarious learning from others, receiving peer feedback, or developing peer support relationships. Nevertheless, most patients prefer the individual attention they may receive in this format.

We have also found that the duration of the CBT treatment, which includes eight modules, can range from eight to fourteen sessions. Certain modules, because of their length, may require more than one session. Individual patients may vary in their pace or comfort in the length of the treatment session. You must keep in mind that it will take longer for the group format to complete CBT for co-occurring disorders.

Although each clinician will have his or her own sequence for conducting each CBT session, we suggest using the following sequence when conducting a CBT session for an individual with co-occurring disorders:

1. Begin each session with an inquiry about substance use, psychiatric symptoms, crises, and treatment attendance since the last session.

2. Conduct a brief review of the previous session's content and ask a few questions to evaluate the patient's comprehension and understanding of the material.

3. Review the patient's practice/homework. Reinforce all attempts at adherence and emphasize the importance of homework in learning new skills.

Individual patients may vary in their pace or comfort in the length of the treatment session.

4. Present a brief overview of the current session's content. Use examples and demonstrations.

5. Ask open-ended questions about the material to assess comprehension (e.g., "Today, we talked about the type of treatment we'll be doing. What is your understanding about what we'll be doing?"). Clarify as needed. Note areas of particular difficulty or confusion for future review.

6. When introducing new material, ask the patient for examples of how this information pertains to him or her. Ask the patient to identify how—and perhaps demonstrate how—the new skill or information can be directly applied to his or her situation.

7. Review any new material from the session.

8. Assign practice work for the next session.

9. Close the session by asking what was helpful and what was not helpful.

10. Affirm and support the patient's progress and continuation; confirm the date and time of the next session.

Each module in this curriculum contains some common elements. They are

- stated goals for each module
- time required, including additional sessions when needed, and handouts
- suggested steps for each session
- practice/homework for patients
- clinical observations for the clinician's evaluation tool
- therapeutic alliance

Group Sessions

Driven both by tradition and financial pressures, most addiction treatment takes place in group formats. This curriculum can be used in the group format, but the clinician and co-clinicians of groups should keep in mind some important items.

Commonality and Cohesiveness

The same factors associated with the therapeutic alliance and therapeutic frame apply equally to the conduct of group therapy and perhaps even more so. Clinicians must work to set the tone for commonality at the outset. For example, it will be important to establish the reason for the group. This reason may need to be stated plainly, such as "We are going to be working on problems associated with both drugs or alcohol and mental health issues." The starting assumption is that everyone in the group at least has questions if not psychiatric and substance use disorders. Thus the clinician needs to communicate from the outset what the criteria are for referral or membership in the group.

Another key issue is that patients will have varying problems with substance use and psychiatric disorders. (For example, the type of disorders, the severity of disorders, and patients' stage of motivation will vary.) The clinician may need to ask participants to recognize the differences, but also understand that more gains will be made if they all focus on the similarities. A good group clinician will foster the sense of identification and commonality by making connections between statements made by group members.

Cohesiveness is an essential component to a good group experience. The feeling that participants "are in this together" is core to the group's trust and potential for growth. The clinician will need to attend to factions within the group. The clinician also needs to foster a sense of safety, confidentiality, mutuality, and common purpose.

The common purpose of CBT for co-occurring disorders is based on a desire to learn about substance use and psychiatric disorders—and how they interact—to make recovery work. Clinicians would also hope to teach patients new ways to reduce anxiety (via breathing retraining) and new coping skills (to replace the maladaptive "skill" of using substances to deal with symptoms).

Group Norms

Group norms or rules will need to be established. Typically these are communicated in individual sessions prior to a patient starting a group. Sometimes group rules are printed up creatively and posted on the wall of the group room or provided to a patient as a handout upon referral to the group. These norms may also be communicated by the clinician during the course of the group, particularly as issues are raised.

Cohesiveness is an essential component to a good group experience. The feeling that participants "are in this together" is core to the group's trust and potential for growth.

Certain ground rules for group behavior should be addressed. Some topics may include punctuality and consequences for being late; providing feedback or "cross-talk"; contact with the clinician or other group members between sessions; use of language (such as profanity); bringing food, drinks, or cellular phones; and consequences for certain behaviors.

Most programs and clinicians who will be using CBT in group formats likely have group norms and rules already developed. CBT can be readily implemented within most existing group formats.

Structure

Every clinician may have his or her own unique approach to conducting CBT for co-occurring disorders in a group format. This may vary by the mix of patients, the size of the group, the type of room, the nature of the program, and, of course, the experience and style of the group clinician.

We suggest using the following sequence for CBT for co-occurring disorders in groups:

1. Welcome patients to the group session.

2. Inform patients about any clinician vacations or administrative or therapeutic frame changes.

3. If new members are present, have introductions.

4. Check with patients about substance use, crises, and other treatment compliance matters. (This should be kept to a minimum.)

5. Answer questions from the previous session.

6. Check the practice work assigned at the previous session (homework).

7. Present the current module title and purpose.

8. Use an example or demonstrate the skill.

9. Ask patients to work on the skill on their own.

10. Depending on the group, you may want to ask each member to share his or her experience, or ask for volunteers to share their experiences. (Be attentive to drawing in those who tend not to share.)

11. Depending on the group, you may want to ask patients to provide feedback to each other. (Emphasize supportive and affirming feedback.)

12. Review any new material from the session.

13. Assign practice work for the next session.

14. Close the group by asking what was helpful and what was not helpful.

15. Affirm and support patients' progress and continuation; confirm the date and time of the next session.

Whether it is used in group or individual formats, this curriculum will be a guide for application of each module into clinical practice. No two clinicians will implement this curriculum in precisely the same way. We expect the first patient or the first group to be your "test case" and for you to get better at your own style and approach with each successive application. In other words, practice and repetition is good for clinicians and patients alike!

3. Session Structure

Although the session length is flexible, this guide is written with a forty-five- to fifty-minute session in mind for individual formats. It is possible to end early if necessary. Let the patient's attentiveness and engagement guide you. For group formats, sixty- to ninety-minute sessions are appropriate. The more patients with severe psychiatric disorders (such as severe bipolar disorder, schizophrenia, or schizoaffective disorders), the shorter the sessions will need to be. Though eight modules comprise the CBT program, it is likely that the clinician may need up to fifteen sessions to complete the program in its entirety.

4. Practice

Homework, or practice, is an important part of therapy, particularly during the cognitive-restructuring phase. Recent research has found that patients who do homework have better outcomes in CBT than patients who don't. The importance of working on homework should be emphasized without being punitive. Early in therapy, during the patient education modules, worksheets can be done (or at least started) in the session together. The patient's homework would be to review them, add to them, and practice breathing retraining. During cognitive restructuring, the patient will be completing homework himself or herself. This gradual approach can help shape participation over time. Some patients may be very sensitive to the "academic" aspect of homework. Homework may remind them of prior difficulties in school, stimulate evaluation anxiety, or reveal educational deficits or illiteracy. The clinician is advised to be tuned into these matters and be comfortable in discussing patients' concerns. If illiteracy is an issue, the treatment can still be conducted by relying on verbal repetition.

5. Plan and Duration

The plan and duration concerns the various modules, number of sessions to cover the modules, and the number of sessions overall. This curriculum is organized by eight successive modules: (1) Introduction to CBT, (2) Substance Relapse and Crisis Prevention Plan, (3) Breathing Retraining, (4) Patient Education I: Primary Symptoms of Co-occurring Disorders, (5) Patient Education II: Associated Symptoms of Co-occurring Disorders, (6) The Five Steps of Cognitive Restructuring: The First Three Steps, (7) Cognitive Restructuring: The Five-Step Program, and, finally, (8) Generalization and Beyond.

In addition, twenty reproducible handouts are integrated as practice, or homework, for patients in the above eight modules. For your convenience, the handouts appear on the program CD-ROM.

The therapeutic pace is essentially flexible and set by the patient and clinician. The clinician may need to attend to patient response, capacity, tolerance for frustration or emotionality, and possibly external factors. Individual sessions may go by more quickly, depending on the patient; however, it may also be possible to extend individual sessions to increase the amount of repetition and practice the patient can have (with the clinician's assistance). By necessity, the group format may go by more slowly to accommodate each member's own progress and the amount of exchange between members and from multiple patients to clinician(s). However, it is also equally likely the group format will need to be more structured, less flexible, and afford patients less time for repetition and practice. Only after you implement CBT in your setting and with your particular clientele will you be able to gauge the duration of the program and the time needed to cover each module.

Use the Clinician Checklist (included with the Supervisor Checklist on the CD-ROM) to track the number of sessions used to cover the modules per case you treat. Figure 2 depicts an approximate and suggested outline, with margin for flexibility, for the number of sessions and the duration of treatment by module.

FIGURE 2

Session Outline Tables

Session Outline Table for Individual Sessions

MODULE	INDIVIDUAL SESSION(S) REQUIRED
Modules 1–3 Introduction to CBT, Substance Relapse and Crisis Prevention Plan, Breathing Retraining	1
Module 4 Patient Education I: Primary Symptoms of Co-occurring Disorders	1–2
Module 5 Patient Education II: Associated Symptoms of Co-occurring Disorders	1–3
Module 6 The Five Steps of Cognitive Restructuring: The First Three Steps	1–2
Module 7 Cognitive Restructuring: The Five-Step Program	2–4
Module 8 Generalization and Beyond	2
Total number of modules: 8	Total number of sessions: 8–14

Session Outline Table for Group Sessions

MODULE	GROUP SESSION(S) REQUIRED
Modules 1–2 Introduction to CBT, Substance Relapse and Crisis Prevention Plan	1
Module 3 Breathing Retraining	1
Module 4 Patient Education I: Primary Symptoms of Co-occurring Disorders	1–2
Module 5 Patient Education II: Associated Symptoms of Co-occurring Disorders	1–2
Module 6 The Five Steps of Cognitive Restructuring: The First Three Steps	1–2
Module 7 Cognitive Restructuring: The Five-Step Program	2–5
Module 8 Generalization and Beyond	2
Total number of modules: 8	Total number of sessions: 9–15

Summary

Each clinician must carefully consider five very important aspects in using this curriculum: context, format, session structure, practice, and, finally, the plan and duration of the sessions. Whether delivered individually or in groups, the following eight modules and twenty corresponding reproducible handouts complete the CBT curriculum for co-occurring disorders.

Before proceeding to part II and the patient modules, it is recommended that you first review chapter 6. Though this chapter may be more helpful *after* you have spent time working CBT and CR with patients, we recommend reading this chapter before you begin teaching CR in order to familiarize yourself with potential problems that might arise.

•   •   •

Special Issues with CBT and Co-occurring Disorders

Clinicians typically encounter obstacles when doing CBT and with teaching cognitive restructuring (CR) to patients with co-occurring disorders. This chapter describes different strategies for addressing these common obstacles. These strategies for overcoming certain problems or issues are applicable whether you are conducting these modules individually or are using a group format. This chapter is presented here to help you to anticipate some potential challenges in conducting CBT for persons with co-occurring disorders. These challenges may or may not occur in your clinical work. However, in our experience, this list of potential "problems" is not atypical. This chapter will be more helpful after you have spent time working CBT with patients. However, we recommend reading this chapter before you begin teaching CR in order to familiarize yourself with potential problems and issues that might arise, and reviewing this chapter after you gain more experience teaching CR to patients. Some handouts that you will use later in the sessions are referred to in this chapter.

ISSUE:

Patient Cannot Achieve Stable Abstinence or Wishes to First Develop Coping Skills through CBT to Achieve Abstinence

CBT for co-occurring disorders is perhaps best suited for a patient who is either in addiction treatment—where he or she is abstinent or at least in a controlled environment—or in stable or advanced recovery in a mental health treatment setting in the community. Such treatment will help the patient meet various needs and life challenges, such as the need for psychotropic or addiction medication. CBT can then be targeted and focused. The more that CBT treatment must take on other objectives, the more likely it will be diluted and extended. More time may need to be focused on addiction-related issues and current life-stressor problem solving in the addiction treatment or mental health program.

Results from studies of CBT for co-occurring disorders with patients who are actively using substances are not yet available. (Data are presently being gathered.) For patients to receive maximum benefit from CBT, they should be abstinent. If patients are using, use without harm (as in medication-assisted recovery programs) may be possible; however, if patients are using to the level of a substance use disorder, attending sessions while under the influence, going through withdrawal, using compulsively and impulsively, or using even though their use places them or others in harm's way, then they may require a more intense level of care in a hospital or residential setting.

ISSUE:
Successfully Challenging a Thought Leads to Only Very Small Reductions in Distress

It is common for patients who are learning CR to experience only small reductions in distress after they have successfully challenged a thought. This can be discouraging. There are several strategies for dealing with the apparently small effects of CR on reducing distress.

First, it is important for you to determine whether the patient experiences *any* reduction in distress following the successful challenge and modification of an inaccurate or unsupported thought. To determine this, teach patients how to rate their distress on a 0 to 100 scale, in which 0 equals "no distress" and 100 equals "extreme distress." Have patients rate their initial distressing thought using this scale. Afterward, have patients provide another rating for their modified thought. If a patient believes that the evidence does not support the initial thought and modifies it with a new and more accurate thought, some reduction, however minor, in overall distress should be expected. When the expected reduction in distress occurs, you and the patient can focus attention on this improvement. You should point out that greater improvement will follow after more practice with CR. Reinforcing the patient's efforts in reducing his or her distress, no matter how small, gradually shapes the patient's ability to use CR.

It is possible that a patient may conclude that a new thought is not associated with any reduction in distress. Then you should help the patient compare the two thoughts to verify whether the second, more accurate thought does, in fact, cause a reduction in distress.

A patient's thoughts are typically inaccurate because they involve exaggerated styles of thinking, such as catastrophizing, overgeneralization, and jumping to conclusions.

A patient's thoughts are typically inaccurate because they involve exaggerated styles of thinking, such as catastrophizing, overgeneralization, and jumping to conclusions; therefore, successfully challenging such thoughts usually leads to at least some reduction in distress. You should help a patient compare the distress associated with a more accurate thought to that of a less accurate thought.

If a patient does conclude that a new, accurate thought causes no reduction in distress, then you can recruit the patient's help in reconciling this contradiction. You can feign puzzlement, scratch your head, and ask the patient to explain how an inaccurate belief that is *not* supported by evidence is as distressing as a more accurate thought that *is* supported by the evidence. This approach can shift the weight away from the clinician trying to "prove" to the patient that CR works. Instead, let the patient explain how examining and challenging inaccurate thoughts related to distressing feelings can, in fact, have no effect on those feelings.

ISSUE:
Patient Clings to Beliefs of Excessive Self-Blame or Unduly Perfectionistic Expectations

To help a patient accurately evaluate evidence for and against his or her beliefs, it is common to ask the patient to judge how another person might have behaved in the same situation. You might ask the patient, "What would another person's responsibility be had he or she experienced the same event?"

Often when patients are asked to imagine how another person might think and behave in a similar situation, patients do not hold that person as responsible or blameworthy as they hold themselves. Some patients have unduly high expectations of themselves. When asked whether other people would hold such high expectations for themselves, these patients may acknowledge that they would not. Such people, they think, would not be to blame for adhering to "lower standards."

This strategy is often effective at encouraging patients to examine their own beliefs about their responsibility for events and their self-imposed perfectionistic standards.

However, on occasion, some patients cling to greater personal responsibility and perfectionism, even while frankly acknowledging that these standards are at variance with (greater than) others' standards. In these circumstances, ask the patient the reason for this difference. "What makes you so special?" or "Why should you be held to higher standards of behavior?" are ways of questioning a patient who holds himself or herself up to an unreasonably higher standard of

Duplicating this page is illegal. Do not copy this material without written permission from the publisher.

33

behavior than other people (and, as a result, carries much more self-blame). Ask if his or her standards and reasons are rational and justified.

Some patients say, "I should be more responsible," or "I should achieve higher standards of perfection than other people." Implicit in these statements is the belief that the patient *is* better or *is capable of being* better than other people. Both of these assumptions should be challenged. It's possible that a patient holding himself or herself to a higher standard of perfection than others is avoiding responsibility by finding himself or herself blameless when such unreasonable goals are not achieved.

Beliefs about excessive responsibility or perfectionism may be related to patients' learning experiences when growing up. As children, patients may have been told that they should be more responsible, achieve higher standards of perfection, and be better than other people. In their natural desire to please others, these patients often openly accept what they are told. Ask patients to identify those past experiences that may have led to unrealistic expectations of personal responsibility and perfection. This gives patients the opportunity to directly challenge the basis for those beliefs.

ISSUE:

**Patient Clings to Beliefs That He or She "Knows"
Are Not Supported by Any Evidence**

Sometimes a patient may review the evidence for and against a particular belief and acknowledge that the evidence does not support the belief. For example, a patient may realize that no reasonable evidence supports his belief that he must be an exceptional straight-A student in school. Nevertheless, the patient clings to this belief and has difficulty letting it go. A lower grade of a B in a class depresses him. This patient may helplessly say, "Even though I know it isn't true that I have to have straight As, it still *feels* true," or "I know it isn't true, but I can't help coming back to the thought again and again that I should have As in every subject." He may also say, "I know the evidence doesn't support it, but I still think it's true."

There are several strategies available for addressing thoughts like these that persist despite the absence of evidence supporting such thoughts. First, you can point out to the patient that his or her thoughts and beliefs have been negatively reinforced over many years. As a result, you can explain, "It takes practice and persistence to change those strongly held beliefs."

Assure the patient that repeatedly challenging and replacing ineffective thoughts with more accurate ones will gradually feel more natural and routine. This reassurance normalizes the fact that when patients successfully challenge an old thought they've held for a long time with a new one, the new thought does not automatically *feel* real. This is a normal part of changing one's own thinking. The "realness" of the new beliefs will gradually take root as the patient develops new ways of thinking.

A second approach to this problem is to help patients distinguish between what *feels* right or correct and what *is* correct. A belief may *feel* right, but that doesn't make it right. Explain how a belief that feels correct may not be supported by available evidence or be correct in objective analysis. Help the patient recognize this thinking pattern as a common style of thinking called "emotional reasoning."

It is not unusual for patients who have thought a particular way for a long period of time to continue to feel that those thoughts are correct even in the face of counterevidence or contradiction. Acknowledging that long-held beliefs may continue to "feel right," even after they have been successfully disputed, normalizes this experience. It helps patients understand that over time—as they are able to replace inaccurate and unhelpful thoughts and beliefs with more accurate and adaptive ones—their new beliefs will eventually come to "feel normal."

A third approach may be helpful for patients who cling to ineffective beliefs despite repeated attempts to let those beliefs and thoughts go. This approach involves constructing a "payoff matrix" (also known as a functional analysis) aimed at understanding what the patient gains in continuing to hold on to his or her belief. Using the payoff matrix, patients identify the costs of giving up that belief.

Constructing a payoff matrix assumes that adhering to a belief that is unsupported by evidence serves an important function in the person's life. It is not illogical or irrational to hold on to these negative beliefs. Constructing a payoff matrix helps you identify the patient's perceived costs and benefits of holding on to an old and inaccurate belief versus

To view an example of such a matrix, refer to handout 20, Payoff Matrix, which is located on the CD-ROM. Print this handout and use it whenever necessary with your patients during sessions.

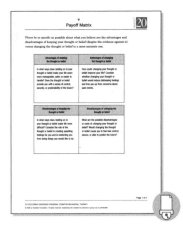

Duplicating this page is illegal. Do not copy this material without written permission from the publisher.

35

changing that belief to a more accurate one. Once the costs and benefits have been identified, those perceptions can be the focus of further attention.

When constructing a payoff matrix, you create a table with four rows and two columns. The first box in the first column contains a heading that corresponds to the advantages of a patient keeping or holding on to the belief in question, and the first box in the second column contains a heading that corresponds to the advantages of changing the belief or thought.

In addition, the third box in the first column is a heading associated with disadvantages of keeping a thought, and the third box in the second column refers to the disadvantages of changing a thought. You then work with the patient to identify

1. the advantages of keeping or holding on to the thought (second box in column 1),

2. the disadvantages of keeping or holding on to that thought (last box in column 1),

3. the advantages of adopting the new thought (second box in column 2) and, finally,

4. the disadvantages of giving up the old thought and adopting the new one (last box in column 2).

Having identified these advantages and disadvantages, you and your patients can then mutually explore and challenge some of these perceptions. Specifically, you may help patients challenge the perceived benefits of holding on to or giving up a particular belief. Realizing the high cost some patients pay for holding on to certain beliefs can be beneficial.

Assume a collaborative stance with the patient. Help him or her understand the benefits of holding on to certain beliefs compared to the costs of giving up those beliefs. For example, one patient continued to believe that she was somehow responsible for the sexual abuse she experienced in childhood. One advantage of clinging to this belief was that it gave her an illusion of control. If she was partly or even wholly responsible for her own sexual abuse, then she might have greater control in preventing such events from happening in the future. The greatest disadvantage of holding on to that belief was that she felt bad about herself when she had intrusive memories of her childhood sexual abuse.

She identified that the primary advantage of accepting the belief that she was not responsible for her abusive experiences was better self-esteem. The primary disadvantage of giving up responsibility was that the world seemed scarier, less predictable, and less under her control. Examining these advantages and disadvantages helped her identify and challenge the more fundamental belief that "the world is an extremely unpredictable and dangerous place." After analyzing her thoughts in the payoff matrix, she could retain or change her thoughts, which allowed her to make informed choices based on the perceived advantages and disadvantages of each alternative. Such an analysis illustrates to patients the price they pay for adhering to unrealistic beliefs concerning responsibility for traumatic events.

When conducting a payoff matrix, you will find that for patients one of the most common disadvantages of giving up unrealistic thoughts or beliefs about control or responsibility over events lies within accepting a view of the world that recognizes a certain amount of unpredictable risk and danger. Some patients may experience relief when they are able to develop more realistic perceptions of risk and danger. However, some patients experience high levels of anxiety when they perceive there to be *any* risk, and this anxiety may serve as a barrier to developing more realistic perceptions.

In these circumstances, rather then attempting to modify a patient's perceptions of risk, it is preferable to help the patient accept that level of risk in the world. The patient may need to understand and accept that a certain amount of risk in living is inescapable. To get on with his or her life, the patient needs to work on accepting the risks he or she faces on a day-to-day basis and is likely to face in the future. Patients who accept this risk can then be helped to modify their beliefs concerning excessive control over or responsibility for past and future events.

For patients who absolutely cannot accept this degree of risk, the clinician can focus the discussion on exploring possible lifestyle changes that might reduce those perceptions of risk even further. However, these patients will need a great deal of help in learning that no one can escape all risks.

To get on with his or her life, the patient needs to work on accepting the risks he or she faces on a day-to-day basis and is likely to face in the future.

Duplicating this page is illegal. Do not copy this material without written permission from the publisher.

37

ISSUE:

**Patient Has Difficulty Learning the Five Steps of CR or Reports
That the Skill Is Too Burdensome and Needs to Be Simplified**

Patients do not have to learn all five steps of CR to learn the essence of the skill. There are two general strategies available for helping patients learn and apply CR. These strategies can be used in combination with each other.

First, the greater the difficulty the patient experiences in learning the steps of CR, the more important it is to involve others to help the patient use CR skills outside the session. These individuals can include case managers, family members, friends, spouses, or other caring people. You can review the CR steps with these individuals. In turn, they can help the patient use the skill in appropriate situations where the patient might otherwise forget to use the skill. The use of significant others to help patients learn the steps of CR may be especially valuable among patients with cognitive impairments. These patients may experience difficulties with spontaneous generalization of the skills from the session to their day-to-day experiences.

Second, try explaining the steps of CR in three basic steps:

1. Recognize the feeling.

2. Identify the bad thoughts (inaccurate or exaggerated thoughts) leading to the upsetting feeling.

3. Change the thought (by asking if there is another way of looking at a situation or thought).

A slight variation on these three steps is

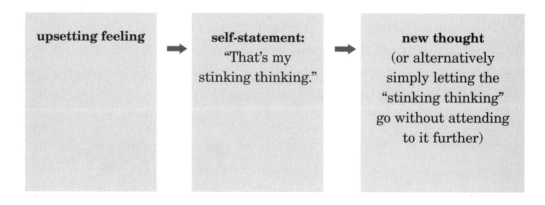

upsetting feeling → **self-statement:** "That's my stinking thinking." → **new thought** (or alternatively simply letting the "stinking thinking" go without attending to it further)

Thus, in simplifying CR, the most critical step of the skill is helping patients understand that when they experience distressing feelings there are thoughts that underlie those feelings. Those thoughts need to be challenged, changed, or ignored to minimize or change the upsetting feelings that result.

ISSUE:
Patient Reports Being Unable to Use CR in the Moment

If the patient has difficulty using CR when he or she is actually upset, ask the patient if he or she is able to use CR at other times, such as during the session or at the end of the day when completing the homework assignment.

To do CR in the moment, the patient first needs to be able to do CR at some other more relaxed time. For many, it takes time to learn how to do CR during actual distressing moments. The challenge of doing CR in the moment should be considered a skill that patients will learn through extensive practice.

Some patients are capable of doing CR in session and at the end of the day; however, you need to ask the patient if he or she is able to recognize an upsetting emotion in the moment as a cue for initiating CR. If not, help the patient focus and learn how to recognize these emotions as a cue for CR.

If the patient is able to recognize an upsetting emotion as a cue but has difficulty identifying the thoughts or beliefs underlying that emotion in the moment, focus on identifying relevant thoughts by reviewing them in the session with handouts. Both the recognition of distress as a cue for initiating CR and the identification of thoughts and beliefs underlying distressing emotions can be role-played in the session.

Some patients may be able to immediately recognize upsetting emotions as a cue for initiating CR and to identify an appropriate thought. However, they may have difficulty generating and weighing the evidence for and against that thought.

Then, a helpful shortcut is to prompt the patient (and practice in session) to identify whether the thought reflects a common style of thinking which can then be immediately altered. Identifying common styles of thinking is a useful shortcut to the more laborious steps of CR of generating evidence and formally evaluating whether the evidence supports the thought. If a patient is unable to utilize common styles of thinking to challenge thoughts experienced in the moment, this should be the primary focus of training, both in the session and for homework. Handout 14 is specifically aimed at helping patients identify common styles of thinking. (The handout can be found on the CD-ROM.)

ISSUE:

Patients with PTSD Report Being Able to Use CR to Address Everyday Stressors, but Not to Address Trauma-Related Distress

Trauma-related distress is often the most difficult distress for people to address. The challenge of using CR to address it should be normalized for patients. Trauma-related distress can be addressed in therapy sessions, especially early in treatment when patients are learning CR. These patients should be reassured that they will become more and more skillful at using CR and as a result be more able to address trauma-related distress on their own.

To help patients learn how to address trauma-related distress on their own, first work on trauma-related issues in sessions. Extend this work to home practice after part or all of the CR training is conducted in the session. Increasingly larger chunks of trauma-related distress work can be given to patients to practice on their own as homework assignments under controlled conditions. As patients become more able to address trauma-related distress on their own through practice in homework assignments, their ability to use CR to address spontaneous trauma-related distress will also increase. The ability to handle trauma-related distress is gradually shaped by giving the person increasingly difficult assignments to address this distress through CR as homework.

ISSUE:

Patient Is Uncertain about Which Situations to Work On with CR

You should encourage the patient to use CR whenever he or she experiences distressing emotions. These emotions may occur in specific situations or seem to occur spontaneously. It doesn't matter in which "situations" the patient uses CR. Rather, what is important is that the patient views upsetting emotions as a cue for using CR to evaluate and examine whether the thoughts and beliefs behind the emotions are supported by objective evidence.

Trauma-related distress is often the most difficult distress for people to address.

ISSUE:

Patient Reports an Inability to Generate Evidence against a Thought

Consider resolving this issue by determining whether the patient can generate evidence in these three situations: (1) during sessions, (2) with homework, and, finally, (3) in the moment.

During Sessions

First ask the patient whether he or she is able to generate evidence against certain thoughts during sessions. If not, you should help the patient learn how to do this work in the session by identifying easy exaggerated thoughts related to distressing emotions and prompting him or her to identify evidence against those emotions. You should provide hints at first for possible evidence against specific thoughts, but then shift responsibility for identifying evidence to the patient.

With Homework

Once the patient is able to generate evidence against thoughts in the session, homework assignments can be provided. These homework assignments should gradually increase in difficulty. Begin with very exaggerated thoughts that were identified in the session and list one or two pieces of evidence (which were already furnished) against those thoughts. The patient's homework or practice is to generate more evidence against the thoughts. As the patient becomes more able to generate evidence against thoughts in controlled homework assignments, increase the amount of CR work.

In the Moment

If the patient is successful doing CR in the session and for homework assignments but has difficulty doing CR in the moment, consider rehearsing breathing retraining as a strategy for relaxing the patient. This can calm the patient, giving him or her a better chance to identify evidence in the moment. If the patient still has difficulty generating evidence against the thought, consider practicing with him or her until he or she is able to identify the common style of thinking that characterizes the thought.

Duplicating this page is illegal. Do not copy this material without written permission from the publisher.

41

ISSUE:

Patient Reports an Inability to Identify Automatic Thoughts

If patients are able to identify upsetting emotions appropriate for CR, but have difficulty identifying the automatic thoughts or beliefs underlying those emotions, do further practice with them to help them identify those thoughts. This practice can be guided by handout 13, Guide to Thoughts and Feelings, and should be done in the session, followed up by homework assignments focusing just on the identification of thoughts and beliefs underlying distressing emotions. (The handout is located on the CD-ROM.)

ISSUE:

Patient Can Generate an Alternative Thought but the Degree of Believability Is Low

This problem probably involves situations in which the patient has concluded that the evidence does not support a particular belief and thus an alternative thought or belief is called for. If the evidence *does* support a particular belief or thought, the patient should be prompted to come up with an action plan to deal with that concern and the upsetting emotion associated with it. If the patient can generate a new thought to replace the older inaccurate thought but does not find the new thought very "believable," he or she should be encouraged to come up with a new thought that incorporates some of the evidence against the old thought.

Since the patient has already concluded that the evidence does not support his or her old thought, it is critical that the evidence used to challenge the old thought is reflected in some way in the new thought. Encourage the patient to talk about the evidence to prompt a more realistic appraisal of the situation. The overall believability of the new thought is important. It is most critical that the new thought is believed more than the old one. The fact that the new thought doesn't seem real or believable may reflect the newness of the thought rather than its objective credibility.

When helping patients identify more accurate thoughts, it is important for you not to actually supply those thoughts. Instead, use questions to prompt the patient to identify the thought that he or she is most likely to find believable. There are two levels of believability: factual believability and emotional believability. As long as the person finds the thought factually believable (i.e., the thought is in line with the evidence), the patient should be encouraged to stick with that thought. Then strategies should be developed for the patient to practice and remind himself or herself of that thought.

Many identify an alternative thought that is factually believable, but it does not seem emotionally believable. That is, the thought may not feel right even though the patient believes it to be more accurate. Such experiences should be normalized. Patients should be informed that it often takes repeated practice until new thoughts and beliefs are incorporated and believed at an emotional level. You can explain to the patient that the old thoughts and beliefs have been reinforced over many, many years, and that it takes time and practice for the new thoughts to replace the old ones and feel right.

ISSUE:
Patient Reports Multiple Thoughts and Feelings Related to the Same Upsetting Situation and Is Uncertain about Which to Challenge

It is common for patients to describe a flurry of thoughts and feelings experienced in a particular situation. Patients should be informed that this experience is common. To prioritize which thoughts and feelings to work on, the patient should be encouraged first to focus on the most distressing feeling. If the patient reports two strong conflicting feelings, have him or her select one. After the patient selects the stronger feeling, he or she should then identify and focus on the strongest underlying thought associated with that feeling.

ISSUE:
Patient Reports Upsetting Situations That Warrant Both Alternative Thoughts and Action Plans

This is an acceptable and even common outcome of CR that is briefly addressed in this guide. If, when evaluating evidence, the patient concludes that the evidence does not support the thought, he or she is encouraged to identify another thought more consistent with the evidence at hand. After identifying this new thought, evaluate the patient's distress. If the patient experiences significant distress from the new thought (although the amount of distress should be less than to the original thought), an action plan is developed for addressing the problem situation.

For example, consider a patient who rarely drove her car except when absolutely necessary. She was convinced that "driving is a very dangerous activity." In CR, she evaluated the evidence initially supporting this belief and concluded that the evidence wasn't accurate. As a result, she identified a new belief more in line with the available evidence, but also acknowledged the apprehension she still felt about driving. "Even though I feel anxious about driving," she said, "driving is quite safe."

Though the patient reported a significant reduction in her distress related to the new thought that driving is safe, she nevertheless continued to feel anxious. The clinician then worked with the patient to identify a three-step action plan for dealing with her anxiety about driving. This action plan had the patient (1) practice breathing retraining before driving, (2) mentally prepare herself for a trip by going through it in her mind before actually taking the trip, and (3) plan several short excursions to familiarize herself with driving for personal reasons.

The steps of this action plan were developed by the patient in consultation with the clinician. The patient was able to implement them successfully and overcome her fear of driving.

ISSUE:
Patient Can't Generate Distressing Situations
from the Past Week (or Otherwise)

The focus of CR need not only be on distressing situations per se, but also can be on the experience of distressing emotions, especially those that interfere with day-to-day functioning. Encourage patients to identify their upsetting emotions in the past week and to describe what was happening when they experienced those emotions or "situations."

If a patient reports no distressing feelings over the past week, he or she is to be congratulated on a remarkable recovery (or at the very least on a very good week). In such situations, you can explore whether the patient harbors distressing feelings about trauma-related thoughts or situations that have been avoided over the past week and focus CR work on those feelings instead.

Acceptance is quite different from resignation or despair, and involves a realistic appraisal of one's circumstance and a commitment to strive toward one's goals.

ISSUE:

Despite Obvious Effort with CR, Patient (and Clinician) Realize That Some Situations Just Cannot Be Changed, Either in Thought or Action

For help with this problem, refer to handout 19, Serenity, which is located on the CD-ROM. Print this handout and use it whenever necessary with your patients during sessions.

There are a number of circumstances where patients cannot alter, either in thought or in action, situations from their past or even in the present. In these circumstances, the clinician is often in a position to assist the patient in a process of "acceptance." This process will likely be familiar to many patients in addiction treatment as an integral concept in Twelve Step recovery programs. In the Serenity Prayer, acceptance is verbalized in the phrase "to accept the things I cannot change," and this prayer is usually recited at every Twelve Step meeting.

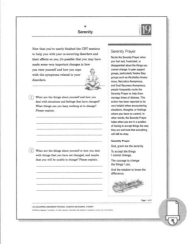

Acceptance is quite different from resignation or despair, and involves a realistic appraisal of one's circumstance and a commitment to strive toward one's goals. Also, acceptance often provides a perspective of humor, irony, or makes the intolerable event seem smaller and more manageable in one's overall life. Newer models of therapy, such as acceptance and commitment therapy (ACT) and mindfulness meditation approaches, begin at this very stage.

• • •

Part II

▼

CBT for Co-occurring Disorders: Therapy Modules

There are eight modules included in this CBT program. You may take anywhere from eight to fourteen sessions (for individual sessions) to complete the eight modules. Some modules are longer and include more handouts than others. Group sessions will take longer than individual sessions. A number of other considerations will need to be evaluated to determine the pace of completing the eight modules. In either case, the following five areas should be addressed from beginning to closure of the program. Keep this list in mind as you conduct the treatment. Since it is a time-limited therapy, it will be important that both you and the patient remember your collaborative purpose and focus.

1. ***Throughout treatment:*** Throughout treatment you clearly communicate to patients that CBT is time limited. Such clear communication is necessary to shape expectations and to motivate patients to make use of the therapy sessions and prepare for the end of treatment. It is also imperative to maintain patients' commitment to care and monitoring for their mental health disorders (that is, patients should continue taking medication if prescribed) as well as be committed to addiction treatment and recovery and maintaining abstinence from all substances (or, in the case of medication-assisted recovery programs, maintaining compliance with all treatment).

2. ***Before or around session 8:*** The treatment termination date is determined jointly by you and the patient. Around session 8, you and other treatment providers may confer to discuss the patient's treatment progress and additional treatment needs, then estimate the number of sessions to treatment completion.

3. ***Before or around session 10:*** You remind the patient again of the time-limited nature of therapy and state the number of sessions remaining. As your patient approaches the end of therapy, it is often a good option to meet every two weeks instead of every week. This will help him or her practice using therapy skills independently before therapy ends. You will taper your contact with the patient toward the end of therapy. Decide with the patient when you will begin meeting every other week.

Elicit input from the patient about his or her view of progress in the therapy to date and what he or she would like to focus on in the remaining sessions. Attend to treatment progress as well as to treatment process. Discuss the patient's concerns about termination. Reassure the patient that you will work together to develop a plan that will help him or her continue to use the skills learned in therapy to manage distress experienced after therapy is over.

4. *One or two sessions before the final session:* Remind the patient of the number of sessions remaining in the therapy. Discuss the process of ending. Reiterate that in the last session you will work together to develop a plan that will help him or her utilize the skills learned in therapy to manage distress after therapy is over.

5. *Final session:* Discuss treatment progress and discharge plan development. Personalize the discussion with specific examples from the therapy and questions relevant to your patient's experience.

• • •

Introduction to CBT

Goals

- Describe cognitive-behavioral therapy (CBT) for co-occurring disorders and give an overview of the eight modules.

- Define co-occurring disorders.

- Introduce the patient to three skills:

    1. breathing retraining

    2. learning about primary symptoms and other issues of his or her co-occurring disorders

    3. cognitive restructuring (CR)

Time

- 10–15 minutes within the 45–50 minutes of an individual session

- 15–20 minutes within the 60–90 minutes of a group session

Handout Needed

- Handout 1: *Introduction to CBT*
  For a thumbnail view of handout 1, see page 115.

▼

Suggested Session Outline

Step 1: Introduce CBT

During the first session you introduce cognitive-behavioral therapy for co-occurring disorders. You may use the paragraphs below as an introduction for each patient you meet with individually or for a group.

We're meeting because you may have co-occurring disorders. A person with co-occurring disorders is someone who has a problem with drugs or alcohol and also has a mental health or psychiatric diagnosis. The treatment we are going to do is especially for people who are trying to get better from both types of problems. It's called cognitive-behavioral therapy, or CBT. You probably already know what kind of mental health issue you have, but we will be reviewing this during our meetings.

In addition, you will be learning about how drugs and alcohol affect your mental health issue, and how your mental health issue affects your addiction and recovery. I intend to help you develop some new skills so that you can deal better with both problems. Today is our first session, and we'll talk about what we will be doing together.

If you are using this program with a group, allow time for each member to briefly share some salient information about himself or herself and especially to identify his or her co-occurring disorders.

Step 2: Introduce the Schedule

This step can be combined with the one above, if desired. It is most important to define the program for the individual or group, including the amount of time for each session and the number of sessions and handouts. In addition, explain the importance of homework, or practice, to the patient and that he or she will be asked to do assignments at home between sessions. It's equally important that patients understand there is a limit and end to the CBT sessions.

The paragraph below is a presentation of the schedule (time limit, number of sessions, and handouts), which can be presented to patients individually. If you are using a group format, this speech can be changed accordingly.

> **We'll attempt to meet once a week for a total of about twelve sessions. Some patients complete the program in as few as eight sessions, but generally there are no more than fourteen. This therapy is time limited, and once we've completed the therapy program, our meetings will end. You will probably have other health care providers who will continue to work with you on other problems, and you will also likely be advised to continue in a number of other activities, including peer support groups, such as Alcoholics Anonymous, Narcotics Anonymous, or Dual Recovery Anonymous, to help you over the long run.**

Remind the patient that there may be an occasion where sessions are not held weekly, but due to progress, scheduling, or other factors some sessions may occur on a twice-per-week or twice-per-month basis. Weekly sessions are best.

Step 3: Present Treatment Overview

Tell the patient (or group) that you will focus on improving his or her skills to manage co-occurring disorders. It may be the case that the patient's counselor and the staff of the patient's addiction treatment program will continue to meet regularly with the patient to work on issues related to the patient's substance use and other areas of his or her life. Inquire if the patient's doctor or other health care provider will continue to meet regularly to work on issues related to his or her psychiatric disorder and substance use.

As a way of introducing the first handout, use the following script:

> **There are three main things we'll work on together that will help with your co-occurring disorders. The first thing we'll do is work on a breathing technique called "breathing retraining." This skill will help you manage anxiety and symptoms of physical tension. Many people with co-occurring disorders have problems with worry, tension, and fear. We'll do breathing retraining first so you can begin using it right away.**

Second, you'll learn about your psychiatric disorder and its primary symptoms. We will also focus on how it affects your substance use. Interestingly, most people with a mental health problem have a problem with alcohol or drugs, and most people with an alcohol or drug problem have a mental health issue. But they seldom ever get treated for both problems, and usually never in the same therapy. This therapy will do that for you. Being aware of and understanding your psychiatric symptoms is an important step toward being able to cope more effectively and get into recovery from both your substance use and mental health disorder.

Finally, I'll teach you a skill called cognitive restructuring. If you have a psychiatric disorder, it probably means you have to deal with many upsetting and distressing emotions. And, as you probably know, these emotions can be difficult to handle. Cognitive restructuring is a skill that will help you deal with the negative emotions that you experience—without using substances.

Step 4: Discuss Handout 1, Introduction to CBT

Discuss handout 1 with the patient. Handouts can be printed out from the CD-ROM. If time allows, you may wish to go into more detail about any of the three main components of the handout, all of which will be the subject of other handouts later. Remind the patient that he or she will be asked to practice breathing retraining, for example, in another session as well as at home between sessions. You may use the following script:

This CBT may be different from other therapy you've had. I will teach you new information and new skills for managing difficult feelings and situations. Because this therapy involves lots of teaching, there may be times when I do most of the talking, especially when I'm teaching you something new. Also, I'll ask you to practice things we work on between sessions. Practice is a very important part of CBT, because it gives you a chance to get better at what you're learning in our sessions.

Step 5: Summarize the Material

A patient may feel overwhelmed at the end of this module, so you may need to reassure the patient (or group). To do this, you may use the following script:

> **It may make you nervous to think about focusing on your psychiatric symptoms and substance use at the same time. That's understandable. Most people are a bit apprehensive to start. Sometimes, talking about your symptoms may even make you feel like using. Experiencing negative emotions without using drugs or alcohol can be a difficult thing to do. Let me reassure you that during these sessions, we'll take things slowly and work together on it. Plus, I'll teach you new skills for handling difficult feelings and situations, and those skills will make this work and any feelings it brings up much more manageable. In fact, if emotions do come up during or after our sessions, it gives us a great opportunity to work on these feelings and to give you new skills to deal with them.**

Step 6: Assign Practice/Homework

No practice/homework is assigned in this module.

Step 7: Write Your Clinical Observations

Ask yourself the following questions to help you evaluate the effectiveness of this module. It might be more insightful if you actually record the answers on a separate sheet of paper.

- Was the diagnosis of a psychiatric disorder or substance use disorder new information for this patient?
- How did the patient respond to your description of the structure of CBT?
- Has the patient had any prior therapy experience? Will this help or interfere with CBT?

Step 8: Complete the Clinician and Supervisor Checklists

In conclusion, review the Clinician Checklist (and, if appropriate, the Supervisor Checklist) found on the program CD-ROM, and record the appropriate information for each patient and/or group.

• • •

Substance Relapse and Crisis Prevention Plan

Goals

- Help the patient identify early warning signs of relapse.

- Encourage the patient to identify feelings prior to use.

- Discuss the patient's relapse prevention plan.

Time

- 10–15 minutes within the 45–50 minutes of an individual session

- 15–20 minutes within the 60–90 minutes of a group session

Handout Needed

- Handout 2: *Substance Relapse and Crisis Prevention Plan*
  For a thumbnail view of handout 2, see page 115.

▼

Suggested Session Outline

Step 1: Review Practice/Homework

Since this module may be covered within the same session as module 1, there is no practice/homework to review at this juncture.

Step 2: Discuss Handout 2, Substance Relapse and Crisis Prevention Plan

Give the patient a copy of handout 2. Discuss numbers one through three on the handout with the patient (or group). Go over the examples given under each number and provide additional ones, if necessary.

Step 3: Have the Patient Complete Handout 2

Have your patient complete the handout at this time. For groups, pencils may be needed, so have plenty on hand. Inquire if anyone in the group has reading or writing difficulties. If so, other arrangements may be needed to accommodate these patients. If meeting with only one patient, you and the patient may decide to complete the handout together, while one of you records the answers.

Step 4: Discuss the Patient's Relapse and Crisis Plan

Initiate a discussion with your patient (or group) about his or her relapse and crisis prevention plan. Use the statements in handout 2 as a guide for your discussion. Reassure the patient that although you will proceed slowly and work together, he or she *may* experience some distress and compulsion to use drugs or drink as he or she talks about or works on his or her negative emotions.

Tell the patient that you want to know about any distress, suicidal thoughts, and/or desires to use that arise during your work together. Reassure the patient that you will work together to manage these feelings. State that one way you can do that is to familiarize yourself with his or her crisis plan. Review the plan the patient has established with other health care providers. (Ensure that you have all the necessary releases in place.)

Reinforce the importance of following the established relapse and crisis prevention plan if the need arises. One analogy that is sometimes useful is the "fire drill." Many patients have been involved in fire drills, either as students or employees, and recognize that this procedure may never be used, but it is important to have in place and be familiar with *just in case*.

Be clear about the protocol regarding whom the patient should contact in the event of a crisis. Consistent with a safety and monitoring plan, it will also be important for you to assess, both directly and indirectly, for adverse or negative reactions to the therapy during the course of treatment.

Step 5: Photocopy Handout 2

After completing and discussing handout 2, make three copies of it. Give one to the patient, place one in the patient's medical record, and keep one yourself. If there is missing information on handout 2, such as phone numbers of a contact person, remind the patient to locate this information and fill it in on the form and relay this information to you at your next meeting.

Step 6: Summarize the Material

Review the goals for this module with your patient (or group). If the patient feels overwhelmed, you may need to offer additional support and reassurance. To do this, you may use the following script:

It may make you nervous to think of relapse. That's understandable. Many patients can feel that way. Sometimes, talking about your symptoms may even make you feel like using. Experiencing negative emotions without using drugs or alcohol can be a difficult thing to do. Let me reassure you that during these sessions, we'll take things slowly and work together on it. Plus, I'll teach you new skills for handling difficult feelings and situations, and those skills will make this work and any feelings it brings up much more manageable. In fact, if emotions do come up during or after our sessions, it gives us a great opportunity to work on these feelings and to give you new skills to deal with them.

Step 7: Assign Practice/Homework

Remind the patient to locate missing information on handout 2 and bring it to your next meeting.

At this juncture, you may be close to finishing session 1, and you will have covered modules 1 and 2. If you can finish module 3, try to do so. If not, ask the patient to complete the remainder of the relapse and crisis prevention plan and bring it to the next session. If the session is coming to an end, also encourage the patient to continue with his or her other treatments and possibly attend peer support group(s) before the next session.

Step 8: Write Your Clinical Observations

Ask yourself the following questions to help you evaluate the effectiveness of this module. It might be more insightful if you actually record the answers on a separate sheet of paper.

- What kind of capacity did the patient demonstrate for identifying triggers to substance use and/or emotional distress?
- What kind of capacity did the patient demonstrate for identifying and labeling thoughts and feelings?
- Does the patient seem connected to other health care providers?
- Does the patient have any non-using social supports outside of treatment providers?

Step 9: Complete the Clinician and Supervisor Checklists

In conclusion, review the Clinician Checklist (and, if appropriate, the Supervisor Checklist) found on the program CD-ROM and in the three-ring binder, and record the appropriate information for each patient and/or group.

• • •

Breathing Retraining

Goals

- Teach the patient the steps to breathing retraining.
- Practice the breathing techniques with the patient in the session.
- Review progress and the therapeutic alliance.

Time

- 10–15 minutes within the 45–50 minutes of an individual session
- 15–20 minutes within the 60–90 minutes of a group session

Handout Needed

- Handout 3: *Breathing Retraining*
  For a thumbnail view of handout 3, see page 115.

▼

Suggested Session Outline

Step 1: Review Practice/Homework

If you ended after module 2, check to see if the patient provided any missing information on handout 2. Also ask if the patient attended treatment and/or peer support group(s) between sessions. Discuss this if appropriate.

Step 2: Introduce Breathing Retraining

Before passing out handout 3, you should first introduce the topic of breathing retraining to the patient (or group). Some clinicians may be very familiar with the topic and comfortable with explaining to patients how to utilize this skill. Others may be less so. To introduce the topic, you can use the following script:

> **The first skill we're going to work on is called "breathing retraining." It's very common for people with co-occurring disorders to experience symptoms of physical tension and anxiety. It's also common for people with substance use problems to have lots of tension and to deal with it by using alcohol or drugs. This new way of breathing can help you deal with and reduce physical tension or anxious feelings. I want to teach you this now so you can begin using it right away.**
>
> **Most of us realize that our breathing affects the way that we feel. For example, when we are upset, we often think of taking a deep breath to calm down; however, taking a deep breath usually isn't helpful. Instead, to calm down one should take a normal breath and exhale slowly. It is exhalation that aids relaxation, not inhalation. While you exhale, say the word "calm," or "relax," or any word that you feel is soothing or that you associate with relaxation. Say the word to yourself very slowly like this: "C-a-a-a-a-a-l-m."**

When suggesting a cue word for relaxation, inquire if the patient has a preference for a specific word. Most people find the words "calm" or "relax" helpful. Check with the patient to see if one of these words is comfortable; occasionally a patient may report that the word "relax" is actually a cue for anxiety. If this is the case, select another cue word.

First, model for the patient how to inhale and exhale through the nose, and then ask the patient to perform the exercise according to the following instructions:

In addition to concentrating on slow exhalation while saying "calm" to yourself, I want you to slow down your breathing. Very often, when people become frightened or upset, they feel like they need more air and may hyperventilate in response to that feeling. Hyperventilation, however, does not have a calming effect. In fact, it causes anxious feelings. Unless we are preparing for a really dangerous situation, we often don't need as much air as we are taking in. When we hyperventilate and take in more air, we signal our bodies to prepare for danger. If we feel anxious and want to calm down, what we really need to do is to slow down our breathing and take in less air.

Step 3: Model the Breathing Technique

Instruct the patient (or group members) to take a normal breath and exhale very slowly while silently repeating the cue word. Some clinicians may ask the patient to close his or her eyes when practicing breathing techniques. However, it isn't necessary. Train the patient to pause and count to four before taking the next breath. Repeat the entire sequence ten to fifteen times with the patient.

Remind the patient that it is important to inhale normally and exhale in a more extended way. You should demonstrate this technique to the patient again.

Some patients will obsess about the cue word, whether to breathe through their nose or mouth, or whether to have their eyes open or closed. You can always tell patients to use whatever approach is most comfortable to them.

Step 4: Discuss Handout 3, Breathing Retraining

Give the patient a copy of handout 3. Remind the patient that you already have instructed him or her on the breathing retraining techniques, and the handout will serve as a reminder to the patient when he or she practices breathing retraining between sessions at home. Summarize the five main steps of breathing retraining with the patient, and inquire if he or she feels confident to do the breathing exercise at home.

Duplicating this page is illegal. Do not copy this material without written permission from the publisher.

63

Step 5: Assign Practice/Homework

Ask the patient to practice breathing retraining twice a day before the next session. Emphasize that practicing the skill on a regular basis when he or she is not distressed (such as when getting up in the morning) will help develop and internalize the skill. Then he or she will be able to use it better in times when it's really needed. Be specific with the patient when discussing times or places that the exercise will be most useful for the patient. Ask when he or she plans to do it during the course of the day. Have the patient commit to the time. Problem-solve about things that might interfere with the exercise. Help him or her find ways to realistically set aside time to practice breathing retraining. Help the patient visualize how to do it within the realities of his or her schedule.

For specific instructions you can use with the patient (or group), use the following script:

> **These breathing exercises work best when you practice them, so try to practice them twice per day. It is also more effective to practice them when you are already relaxed. Breathing retraining is kind of like a fire drill; you learn how to do it when it is not an emergency situation. Then when it is an emergency situation, such as when you feel stress or panic, you will be able to use the skill more automatically.**

Encourage the patient to attend peer support group(s) between sessions.

Step 6: Write Your Clinical Observations

Ask yourself the following question to help you evaluate the effectiveness of this module. It might be more insightful if you actually record the answer on a separate sheet of paper.

- Can the patient demonstrate how to do breathing retraining?

Step 7: Review the Therapeutic Alliance

This is a critical juncture to specifically ask the patient about his or her experience with CBT and about his or her time with you. It is also useful to inquire how the therapy might fit in with his or her other treatment and peer support group participation.

It is also beneficial to affirm the patient's willingness and courage to attend the very first session. He or she undoubtedly had many thoughts of not attending.

In addition, it is important to reinforce two things to the patient:

1. In order to really benefit from the CBT program, the patient will need to stay with it. Remind him or her that research states that patients who stay with the treatment all the way through get better; not only do their psychiatric symptoms improve but also their substance use problems.

2. Getting better is something he or she deserves. This patient has been suffering a great deal with his or her psychiatric symptoms and with substance use. Taking the steps to address the substance use and mental health disorders at the same time says that he or she is worth it.

Step 8: Complete the Clinician and Supervisor Checklists

In conclusion, review the Clinician Checklist (and, if appropriate, the Supervisor Checklist) found on the program CD-ROM, and record the appropriate information for each patient and/or group.

● ● ●

Patient Education I:
Primary Symptoms of Co-occurring Disorders

Goals

- Help the patient understand the nature of the psychiatric symptoms and how they intersect with substance use.

- Review the description and causes of a patient's specific disorder.

- Help the patient conduct an analysis specific to symptoms related to psychiatric problems.

- Help the patient set positive goals.

- Review the therapeutic alliance.

Time

This module may take more than one session to complete.

- 45–50 minutes for an individual session

- 60–90 minutes for a group session

Handouts Needed

- Handout 4A: *Primary Symptoms of Co-occurring Disorders*

- Handout 4B: *Primary Symptoms of the Mental Health Problem*

- Handout 5: *Goals: Positive Psychology*

For thumbnail views of these handouts, see pages 115-116.

From the Fact Sheets, select

- the *Co-occurring Disorders* Fact Sheet

- the appropriate Fact Sheet for the patient's disorder

▼

Suggested Session Outline

Step 1: Review Practice/Homework

Ask the patient if he or she continued to practice the breathing retraining exercise twice a day as instructed. If not, explore any issues the patient may have encountered that prevented him or her from practicing. If the patient did practice, explore the benefits of practice.

Ask the patient if he or she attended peer support group(s) between sessions. Discuss this if appropriate.

Step 2: Discuss Handout 4A, Primary Symptoms of Co-occurring Disorders

Review handout 4A with your patient (or group).

The primary goal of patient education is to help the patient understand the nature of his or her psychiatric symptoms and how they intersect with substance use. Although you will gather important information about the patient's symptoms, the emphasis is on education rather than clinical assessment. Encourage active participation. Ask the patient to describe his or her own experience with the symptoms of his or her disorder and how each symptom applies (or doesn't) to him or her. Some symptoms he or she may "identify" with; the patient may feel that other symptoms do not apply. Make the patient educational material more personally meaningful and, therefore, more memorable. Connect the psychiatric symptoms to substance use. Explain how substance use works, how it helps the patient, how it hurts, and, if possible, help the patient to understand the sequence of events that led to substance use. This will help the patient acquire the CR skill later on. Refer to the handouts and complete them with the patient in the session.

There are ten Fact Sheets specific to psychiatric disorders. They are located on the CD-ROM. There is also one general Fact Sheet about co-occurring disorders. Every patient should receive this Fact Sheet.

The specific Fact Sheets are as follows:

Anxiety and related disorders:

- Generalized Anxiety Disorder (GAD)
- Social Anxiety Disorder
- PTSD
- Panic Disorder
- Obsessive-Compulsive Disorder

Mood disorders:

- Major Depression
- Persistent Depressive Disorder
- Bipolar Disorder

Thought disorders:

- Schizophrenia
- Schizoaffective Disorder

It will usually be clear what Fact Sheet should be used. Patients may have more than one diagnosis, in which case all the Fact Sheets that apply should be distributed. In individual formats, you may insert the appropriate Fact Sheet into the patient workbook in advance. In group formats, you may do the same with each new member of the group, or you may start the group by describing the list of Fact Sheets and having patients select the one(s) that apply to them. The risk here is that patients may not know their diagnosis, so it will be important that they explain how it is they selected a particular Fact Sheet for a psychiatric disorder.

Step 3: Hand Out the Appropriate Fact Sheet and the Co-occurring Disorders Fact Sheet

Once the Fact Sheet on the specific disorder has been distributed, use the following format:

Review the Description of the Specific Disorder with the Patient

Go over the detailed description of the disorder, discussing what it is and what it is not. Go over the basic symptoms. Ask the patient if this description fits with his or her understanding of the psychiatric disorder. It might also be useful to talk about when he or she was first diagnosed and what his or her reaction was.

Duplicating this page is illegal. Do not copy this material without written permission from the publisher.

69

Review the Causes of the Specific Disorder with the Patient

In this segment, it is important to be sure that the patient can talk about his or her understanding of why he or she has the disorder. Attend to matters of guilt or self-blame.

Review the Section Entitled "What Are the Usual Treatments for _____?" from the Fact Sheet

The purpose of this section is to review the treatment the patient has received or is presently receiving for his or her mental health issue. Inquire specifically about treatments the patient may have had pertaining to his or her mental health diagnosis.

Step 4: Discuss Handout 4B, Primary Symptoms of the Mental Health Problem

At this juncture, pass out handout 4B to the patient (or group members). Handout 4B will ask the patient to list the symptoms of the disorder or disorders he or she has. It will also provide the patient a chance to identify which symptoms pertain to him or her and how.

Have the patient fill out handout 4B. You should have already discussed the causes of the patient's disorder with the patient in step 3. However, if the patient hasn't reviewed the causes of his or her disorder, this handout will require him or her to refer to the appropriate Fact Sheet.

Be sure to assess the patient's experience and motivation to deal with his or her psychiatric disorder. You may want to discuss the appropriate use of medications for the psychiatric disorder, attitudes regarding medication use, and other relevant matters. It is important to support the patient's use of appropriate medications, in combination with CBT, as perhaps the best treatment available for his or her co-occurring disorders.

Step 5: Discuss Handout 5, Goals: Positive Psychology

This segment of patient education is focused on positive psychology—helping the person identify goals that his or her symptoms have gotten in the way of. This exercise also is designed to end this module on a positive note, because this part of CBT—focusing on the symptoms and how they apply to the patient—can sometimes be overwhelming to patients. Until patients reach the modules on CR, the only resources they have to rely on are the breathing retraining exercises and their positive expectancy for help from you. Focusing on what they want for themselves is exciting to many patients and adds to their motivation to address the obstacles of their psychiatric disorder.

As a way of introducing this exercise with handout 5, you may use the following script:

> **Many patients seek treatment because they want to eliminate the negative effects of mental health problems from their lives. They want to be less depressed, nervous, out-of-control, isolated, emotionally eviscerated, or angry; however, patients are generally even more motivated to change because of the positive things that will happen for them. Now I want you to think about how your mental health problem has interfered with your life and the things you want for yourself. Examples of some things you may want are a job, relationships, ability to leave the house, sexual relations, or ability to drive a car.**

Pass out handout 5 and walk through the symptoms of the patient's psychiatric disorder. List how each interferes with his or her life, and then have the patient list what things are possible if he or she weren't so bothered by these symptoms. End by listing the three most important things a patient could do if he or she were symptom free. It is important to try to focus on tangible goals. Concrete goals that can be measured, such as behavioral changes or trying new activities, are best.

Step 6: Assign Practice/Homework

This module is flexible and allows you and the patient to decide what to complete together during the session and what to assign as homework. This module may take one or two sessions. Two approaches to homework are possible. The first involves going as far as possible with the primary symptoms of the psychiatric disorder and goals in the first session, and then asking the patient to complete the remainder for homework to be reviewed and discussed in the next session. The second approach is to do an overview of the module and complete one or two symptoms for each disorder cluster and an example of a goal, and then ask the patient to add to the list between visits. The next visit would then involve discussing his or her additions to the handouts.

Encourage the patient to attend other treatment and possibly peer support group(s) between sessions.

Duplicating this page is illegal. Do not copy this material without written permission from the publisher.

71

Encourage the patient to practice breathing retraining twice a day before the next session. Emphasize that practicing the skill on a regular basis when he or she is not distressed (such as when getting up in the morning) will help develop and internalize the skill. Then he or she will be able to use it better in times when it's really needed.

Step 7: Write Your Clinical Observations

Ask yourself the following questions to help you evaluate the effectiveness of this module. It might be more insightful if you actually record the answers on a separate sheet of paper.

- Did the patient make good connections between his or her symptoms and the educational material?
- Does the patient seem to be struggling with issues pertaining to stigma, excessive self-blame or guilt, or minimization?
- Did the patient freely describe the symptoms he or she is presently struggling with?
- What was the patient's emotional response to the material?
- Was the patient able to generate goals? Did you foster some sense of hope for him or her to achieve them?

Step 8: Review the Therapeutic Alliance

In our experience with CBT for co-occurring disorders, delivering this module effectively and completing it with patients is pivotal for patients in determining whether they will either finish or drop out of the treatment. If negative feelings and symptoms are focused on and no specific skills are provided to patients at this stage of the program, then patients may drop out of treatment. We have found three therapeutic alliance strategies to be helpful at this juncture.

First, try to "normalize" a negative emotional response, and affirm a patient's experience and communication of it as *non-avoidant*. Avoidance, although protective, keeps symptoms going. Second, suggest to the patient that the "core" of CBT, CR, is designed specifically to address these negative emotional responses, including avoidance. Last, you can advise the patient that this can be a difficult juncture in the treatment but that it passes quickly. Using the breathing retraining skill is also particularly helpful at this time for patients who have been practicing it.

Step 9: Complete the Clinician and Supervisor Checklists

In conclusion, review the Clinician Checklist (and, if appropriate, the Supervisor Checklist) found on the program CD-ROM, and record the appropriate information for each patient and/or group.

•   •   •

Patient Education II:
Associated Symptoms of Co-occurring Disorders

Goals

- Introduce the most common symptoms associated with psychiatric problems.
- Teach the patient how to deal more constructively with fear and anxiety, sadness and depression, guilt and shame, and anger.
- Help the patient identify important issues in his or her primary relationships.
- Review the therapeutic alliance.

Time

This module may take one to three sessions to complete.

- 45–50 minutes for an individual session
- 60–90 minutes for a group session

Handouts Needed

- Handout 6: *Difficulties Associated with Co-occurring Disorders*
- Handout 7: *Drug and Alcohol Problems*
- Handout 8: *Fear and Anxiety*
- Handout 9: *Sadness and Depression*
- Handout 10: *Guilt and Shame*
- Handout 11: *Anger*
- Handout 12: *Relationship Difficulties*

For thumbnail views of these handouts, see pages 116-118.

▼

Suggested Session Outline

Step 1: Review Practice/Homework

Review the patient's additions to the handouts from the previous session. Ask if the patient attended other treatment and peer support group(s) between sessions. Discuss this if appropriate.

Step 2: Discuss Handout 6, Difficulties Associated with Co-occurring Disorders

Handout 6 introduces this entire module and its handouts to the patient (or group).

This module introduces some other difficulties that people with co-occurring disorders often have. This information can help normalize patients' experiences and serve as a point of engagement into treatment by addressing some of the more tangible things that patients are struggling with. Although substance use is addressed specifically at the outset, the relationship of drug and alcohol use to the psychiatric disorder should be examined in presenting each associated symptom. Other associated symptoms of co-occurring disorders may be less obvious to patients. But if a particular patient does not report having difficulty with a certain associated symptom, do not dwell on that symptom. This module is also important in preparing a patient to address these associated symptoms in CR. The patient learns what the definitions of these symptoms, or effects, are and then begins to think about which ones apply to him or her. He or she will have the chance to "restructure" these effects in modules 6 and 7.

Specific handouts are available for each of the associated symptoms. You may use the following script, though most of the information appears on handout 6:

> **Many people with co-occurring disorders experience other symptoms that interfere with their lives and cause them distress. Let's talk about these associated symptoms. First, people with psychiatric disorders are more likely to have problems with drugs and alcohol. Second, people commonly experience difficulty with four types of negative feelings: fear and anxiety, sadness and depression, guilt and shame, and anger. Third, people who have mental health issues often have difficulty in their relationships with other people and may be**

more likely to have less satisfying relationships. Let's talk about substance use first.

Step 3: Discuss Handout 7, Drug and Alcohol Problems

In this section, first refer the patient back to the Fact Sheet on his or her specific psychiatric disorder. Have the patient read the section entitled "How Does the Use of Alcohol and Other Drugs Affect _____?" Review this content with the patient as a background to handout 7.

Next, refer to handout 7. You can review the narrative on handout 7 with the patient or use the following script:

> **Like you, most people who have a mental health problem also have problems with drugs or alcohol. They may try to avoid their symptoms by using drugs or drinking too much. They may use substances to try to take away the strong negative feelings such as anxiety, sadness, guilt, or anger.**
>
> **Drugs and alcohol can actually make some of these feelings worse over time. Also, because people who have psychiatric disorders often have sleep problems, such as trouble falling asleep or nightmares, they may use drugs or alcohol to try to sleep better. Although this may seem helpful at first, drugs and alcohol interfere with the body's ability to sleep well, and people who use a lot of drugs or alcohol can end up with more sleep problems.**
>
> **So, even though people may use drugs or alcohol to try to feel better, this strategy can have a boomerang effect and can even make things worse. You may have been using drugs and alcohol in this way, so you may know exactly what I am talking about. You may also know that using drugs and alcohol may work in the short run but causes problems in the long run. Plus, the negative feelings and symptoms still return—often with a vengeance.**
>
> **Also, the hardest part of recovery is often dealing with "life on life's terms," including dealing with feelings. Maybe once you stopped drinking or getting high, all the negative feelings returned and you wondered, "Why bother?" This is an important stage to get through, and CBT will be really helpful with this.**

Step 4: Instruct the Patient to Answer Questions in Handout 7

Have the patient complete handout 7, and then review his or her answers carefully in the session. Be sure the patient describes how the use of drugs or alcohol related to his or her psychiatric symptoms does or does not work for the patient. Make sure the patient understands the interaction between substance use and psychiatric symptoms and recognizes the connection between substance use and a self-perpetuating maladaptive coping strategy.

It's important that patients make this connection. Your approach to helping patients understand this connection must be done in an empathic and normalizing manner. In group formats, patients will easily identify with one another on the strategy of using substances to cope with psychiatric symptoms. In individual formats, patients may feel judged by the clinician for engaging in a process so obviously self-defeating.

Step 5: Introduce the Four Handouts on Negative Feelings

After the patient finishes handout 7, introduce the remaining handouts and their corresponding subjects. You may use the following script:

> **We are now going to take a look at several of the most common symptoms of psychiatric problems. These are feelings or emotions that you probably have, or have had at some point in your life. We group them into four categories:**
>
> **• fear and anxiety**
>
> **• sadness and depression**
>
> **• guilt and shame**
>
> **• anger**
>
> **Let's talk about fear and anxiety first.**

Step 6: Introduce Handout 8, Fear and Anxiety

As a way of introducing handout 8, you may use the following script:

> **Fear and anxiety are very common feelings that people with psychiatric disorders have. Physiologically, these feelings are best understood as reactions to a threat or danger. When someone experiences an actual threat, he or she is in real danger. But many people with psychiatric disorders experience strong feelings of fear and anxiety even when they are not in any real danger.**

When have you felt fearful, tense, or anxious? What are these feelings like for you when they happen? When you feel fear and anxiety, you may also experience lots of physical tension and fearful thoughts. The physical tension that goes along with fear can make you feel jumpy, tense, or on guard. And when people feel a lot of fear, they also think fearful thoughts, such as "the world is unsafe," or "I am not safe." Feelings of fear and anxiety are often triggered by things that scare you or things that make you worry that something really bad might happen. Sometimes these fears are about being hurt or harmed, being rejected or abandoned, being shamed or humiliated, or simply being afraid of anxiety itself. What kinds of things usually trigger your fear and anxiety?

Step 7: Have the Patient Complete Handout 8

Have the patient complete handout 8 while he or she is in the session. If necessary, help the patient identify his or her triggers to fear and check those situations that apply specifically to the patient's fears.

Step 8: Discuss Handout 9, Sadness and Depression

Introduce handout 9 to the patient. You can review the narrative on handout 9 with the patient or use the following script:

Other common psychiatric symptoms include sadness and depression. After negative life events (such as a perceived rejection, loss, or failure), people often feel less interested in things and have a hard time having any fun. For some people who suffer from major depression, it may be hard to connect these deep, dark, and negative feelings with anything that happened. It seems as though they are just there. When a person feels this way, it's not all that uncommon to feel hopeless about things or to think a lot about suicide. As we talked about earlier, if you ever feel that way, I want you to tell me so I can help you with those thoughts and feelings.

Have you been feeling sad or depressed? Have you been feeling down, uninterested in things, or hopeless?

Sometimes, sadness and depression can feel so hard to deal with that people start to feel as though they can't deal with anything, or that they will never get over what happened and will never feel any differently, or that they are weak or stupid. Thinking things will never get better and that the negative feelings will never go away leads to feelings of sadness, depression, and hopelessness. So it becomes a vicious downward spiral: sadness and depression may make a person feel like things will always be bad, and this thought adds to increased feelings of sadness and depression.

Do you ever have negative thoughts about yourself or about the future? What kinds of things do you think about?

Step 9: Complete Handout 9

Have the patient complete handout 9 while in the session. If necessary, help the patient identify when he or she experiences being sad or depressed and inquire about those situations that apply specifically to the patient.

Step 10: Discuss Handout 10, Guilt and Shame

Introduce handout 10 to the patient. You can review the narrative on handout 10 with the patient or use the following script:

Other negative feelings that people commonly experience are guilt and shame. Sometimes, people blame themselves in some way for what happened, who they are, where they are, or how they feel. They may even blame themselves for having a psychiatric disorder, which they never asked for. They may think about themselves and come to the conclusion that everything was their fault or that they deserved it. These kinds of beliefs lead to guilt and shame.

Do you ever have feelings of guilt or shame?

People may also feel guilty or ashamed because of the mental health problem itself. In our society, sometimes having a mental health disorder is associated with being unusual, weird, scary, dangerous, or different. Sometimes, when people suffer with these symptoms for a long time, they may come to believe that they are weak, or if they were stronger, they'd be over the psychiatric disorder by now. These kinds of thoughts also lead to guilt and shame.

Do you ever have feelings of guilt or shame about your psychiatric symptoms?

Step 11: Have the Patient Complete Handout 10

Have the patient complete handout 10 while in the session. If necessary, help the patient identify when he or she feels shame or guilt and check those situations that apply specifically to the patient.

Step 12: Discuss Handout 11, Anger

Introduce handout 11 to the patient. You can review the narrative on handout 11 with the patient or use the following script:

> **Feelings of anger are also common reactions to life. People feel angry about what happened to them or angry with the person who harmed them or just angry with no one in particular. Sometimes this anger is stirred up in the presence of loved ones or even strangers. Sometimes people feel angry with themselves because of what happened or because things are not working out the way they want.**
>
> **Have you experienced angry feelings? What kinds of things usually make you angry?**
>
> **At times, the anger can be so strong that people swear, yell, or want to hit someone. These strong feelings can be hard to understand or handle. For other people, there is lots of anger that never comes to the surface or gets expressed. It can feel scary or dangerous to express the anger.**
>
> **Feeling angry often can make it hard to get along with others. Also, lots of anger can lead to the other negative feelings we discussed, including fear, sadness, or guilt.**
>
> **Have you ever struck out at yourself or others because of your anger? Has your anger led to any problems?**

Step 13: Have the Patient Complete Handout 11

Have the patient complete handout 11 while in the session. If necessary, help the patient identify what triggers his or her anger and write about those situations or people in the space provided.

Step 14: Review Handout 12, Relationship Difficulties

Introduce handout 12 to the patient. You can review the narrative on handout 12 with the patient or use the following script:

> **Now I'd like to talk about relationship difficulties. If you have co-occurring disorders, you may not feel as close to others as you'd like. This is in part a result of feeling the negative emotions we discussed earlier, such as fear, anxiety, sadness, guilt, or anger. These feelings can get in the way of feeling close to others. Also, for people with mental health problems, there is often a tendency to withdraw and isolate.**

> **Of course, being around or interacting with others can stir up negative emotions, so sometimes people withdraw from others or do not participate in activities that involve other people. This kind of withdrawal, used to cope with negative feelings, can be confusing to loved ones and may lead to conflicts as they try to understand what's happening.**

> **What kinds of relationship difficulties have you experienced? What has this been like for you?**

> **Sometimes, along with a psychiatric disorder, people experience difficulties in their sexual relationships. They may be less interested in sex because they feel depressed or sad. They may be less interested in sex because they feel anxious or fearful. Or sexual activity may remind them of what happened during a traumatic experience from their past. Sometimes people avoid sex because feeling that kind of closeness can cause feelings of vulnerability or anxiety.**

> **Some people do the opposite. They use sex compulsively, out of anger, and do so in a way that is self-destructive.**

> **Have you experienced any of these kinds of difficulties?**

Do you think these kinds of relationship difficulties make CBT or other treatment difficult for you? Perhaps you are afraid to speak in groups, certain people frighten you, or it is difficult for you to concentrate and sit still.

Do these issues also make attending and participating at peer support group meetings difficult? Is it hard to introduce yourself, to talk with others before or after a meeting, or to ask someone for his or her phone number or to be a sponsor?

Step 15: Have the Patient Complete Handout 12

Have the patient complete handout 12 while in session. If necessary, help the patient identify the relationship problems he or she is experiencing and check those situations that apply specifically to the patient.

Step 16: Assign Practice/Homework

This module is flexible and allows you and the patient to decide what to complete together during the session and what to assign as outside session work. This module may take one to three sessions. Much like in module 4, two approaches to homework are possible. The first involves discussing fear and anxiety and the other symptoms associated with psychiatric disorders as much as possible in the first session of this module and completing the handouts together. The handouts that aren't finished are then assigned as homework to be reviewed and discussed in the next session. The second approach is to do an overview of the module and complete one or two examples per handout, and then ask the patient to add to these handouts before the next visit. The next visit would then involve discussing his or her additions to the handouts.

Encourage the patient to attend planned treatment and peer support group(s) between sessions.

Encourage the patient to continue to practice breathing retraining twice a day before the next session. Emphasize that practicing the skill on a regular basis when he or she is not distressed (such as when getting up in the morning) will help develop and internalize the skill. Then he or she will be able to use it better in times when it's really needed.

Duplicating this page is illegal. Do not copy this material without written permission from the publisher.

83

Step 17: Write Your Clinical Observations

Ask yourself the following questions to help you evaluate the effectiveness of this module. It might be more insightful if you actually record the answers on a separate sheet of paper.

- Was the patient able to identify feelings easily? Did you need to use handout 13 to help? (See page 42 of this guide.)

- What are the primary negative feelings the patient seems to have? Can you anticipate what common styles of thinking (which are discussed in handout 14) he or she uses that cause him or her to experience these feelings?

- Were there any specific themes to the patient's relationship difficulties? Is the patient involved in any unsafe situations or abusive relationships? Do you foresee him or her needing to take action?

- Is treatment participation compromised, either in these CBT sessions or with other treatment providers, because of psychiatric symptoms?

- Does the patient make connections between his or her psychiatric symptoms and substance use? Are these connections based on how he or she started using substances, or now?

- Is the patient currently having difficulty staying clean and sober because of his or her psychiatric symptoms?

Step 18: Review the Therapeutic Alliance

As with module 4, in our experience with CBT for co-occurring disorders, delivering module 5 effectively and completing it with the patient is also pivotal for patients in determining whether they will either finish or drop out of the treatment. If associated symptoms are focused on, but no specific skills are provided to patients to help them deal with these symptoms, then they may drop out. We have found three therapeutic alliance strategies to be helpful at this juncture. First, try to "normalize" a negative emotional response, and affirm the patient's experience and communication of it as *non-avoidant*. Avoidance, although protective, keeps the symptoms going. Second, by introducing the patient to handout 13, Guide to Thoughts and Feelings, you are helping him or her to better identify, label, and communicate his or her emotions. Some clinicians have used handout 14, Common Styles of Thinking, to illustrate how thinking can influence negative feelings. This also serves to prepare the patient for CR. Last, you can continue to suggest to the patient that the "core" of CBT, CR, is designed specifically to address the thoughts behind negative feelings, such as depression, anxiety, guilt, shame, and anger. The next module begins CR.

Step 19: Complete the Clinician and Supervisor Checklists

In conclusion, review the Clinician Checklist (and, if appropriate, the Supervisor Checklist) found on the program CD-ROM, and record the appropriate information for each patient and/or group.

●   ●   ●

The Five Steps of Cognitive Restructuring: The First Three Steps

Goals

- Introduce cognitive restructuring (CR) to the patient.
- Help the patient identify and distinguish feelings and connect them to thoughts.
- Teach the patient to identify common styles of thinking.
- Teach the first three steps of CR.

Time

This module may take more than one session to complete.

- 45–50 minutes for an individual session
- 60–90 minutes for a group session

Handouts Needed

- Handout 13: *Guide to Thoughts and Feelings*
- Handout 14: *Common Styles of Thinking*
- Handout 15: *Cognitive Restructuring (CR): Steps 1, 2, and 3*

For thumbnail views of these handouts, see page 118.

▼

Suggested Session Outline

Step 1: Review Practice/Homework

Review the patient's additions to the handouts from the previous session. Ask if the patient attended other planned treatment and peer support group(s) between sessions. Discuss this if appropriate.

Step 2: Introduce Cognitive Restructuring (CR)

This module is the beginning of the CR component of CBT. After introducing this module and the next, you will spend the rest of therapy working through examples of CR that the patient brings in from his or her life. Patients will bring in a variety of thoughts and feelings, which may or may not be directly related to their psychiatric disorder. It may be difficult to determine the cause or source of these feelings. Some patients with a long history of substance use may need help identifying and labeling feelings. It may have been a long time since the patient's feelings were experienced without the filter of a substance. We recommend focusing on the thoughts and feelings that are most distressing to the patient, regardless of their connection to the psychiatric disorder. Learning to handle any negative emotion better will help reduce relapse risk and also provide better coping tools.

When teaching CR to patients, it is generally better to start off with easier examples or life instances. This way the patient can acquire the basics of the skill in the absence of intense emotionality. Once the patient begins to master the skill, it is possible for him or her to take on more significant and emotionally charged material (e.g., re-experiencing symptoms of PTSD).

To introduce CR to the patient, you may use the following script:

So far, we've worked on two important things that can help you with co-occurring disorders. First, you learned breathing retraining which helps you manage the symptoms of anxiety and physical tension that go along with most psychiatric and substance use disorders. Second, you learned about the symptoms of your psychiatric disorder. When you understand that some of the difficulties you are having are related to your co-occurring psychiatric disorder, you can begin to handle these difficult problems in a better and more straightforward

way. Today, we'll begin working on a skill called cognitive restructuring. We call it "CR" for short. This is a strategy for dealing with the upsetting or negative emotions that you sometimes have.

Step 3: Lead a Discussion on Feelings

To help the patient focus on his or her feelings, you may use the following script:

As we have been talking about, people with co-occurring disorders often experience four different kinds of powerful negative emotions: fear and anxiety, sadness and depression, guilt and shame, and anger. There are lots of other emotions, but we'll focus on these four upsetting feelings because they can be the hardest to handle. Since you have been using drugs or alcohol, it's possible that you've blocked out these kinds of feelings. It's also possible that you have felt them very intensely even while drinking or doing drugs. Which of these four kinds of feelings do you seem to experience most often? What kinds of situations usually lead you to feel these things?

Engage the patient in a brief discussion of his or her various feelings and the situations that typically elicit them. Discuss the four emotions listed under the heading "Feelings" in handout 13, Guide to Thoughts and Feelings.

Step 4: Lead a Discussion on Thoughts

To help the patient focus on his or her thoughts, you may use the following script:

Dealing with these feelings is difficult, and one thing that can help you work through them is understanding where these feelings come from. One of the most important things to understand about upsetting feelings is that they are usually linked to what we think about a particular situation or event. So what we think when something happens largely determines what we feel in that situation. For example, imagine that you're walking down the street and you see a friend, but she doesn't say hello to you. How would you feel if that happened? (Pause for the patient's response.) So you would feel hurt. Okay, that's good—you've identified the feeling. Now, what did you just say to yourself about why your friend didn't say hello? (Pause for the patient's response. Examples are "She must not like me, or "I must have offended her in some way.")

If the patient has difficulty identifying his or her thoughts in the previous situation, normalize this and explore further. For example, you might say, "So you would have been hurt. That's great that you can identify that. Now let's try to figure out what you might have been thinking. What other kinds of situations have been hurtful to you?" After exploring another hurtful situation, ask the patient to describe what was hurtful about that situation. This will help you identify the kinds of thoughts he or she was having in those situations that led to his or her hurt feelings. To further explore this issue, you may use the following script:

Now do you think someone else might have different thoughts about your friend's behavior? Can you think of some of the different things someone else might think if this person didn't say hello? For example, a person might have thought things like, "Oh, she wasn't wearing her glasses and didn't see me," or "I wonder if she's sick?" or "What a rude person." How would you feel if you said any of these other things to yourself? Would you feel different if you thought your friend was sick instead of simply not liking you? Yes, you would. So do you see how different thoughts can lead to very different emotions in any situation?

Step 5: Discuss Handout 13, Guide to Thoughts and Feelings

To introduce handout 13 to the patient, you may use the following script:

Handout 13 lists basic emotions and the kinds of thoughts that lead to these emotions. For example, when you feel afraid, you think you're in danger. When you feel sad, you are probably thinking about loss. And if you're feeling guilty or ashamed, you're thinking about something that you have done that is bad or that somehow you are bad. And anger is related to thoughts that something is unfair. You can use this handout as a guide when you're trying to figure out your thoughts and feelings. You might keep one copy with you and another at home to help you identify your feelings and thoughts anywhere.

Point out to the patient the three major headings—"Feelings," "Ask yourself" (questions), and "Related thoughts"—in handout 13. Remind him or her that the initial process of CR is simple. At this stage, the patient should first identify the feeling, then second ask himself or herself the corresponding questions, and then, finally, identify the thought he or she is having about the initial situation.

In summary, you might ask the patient to (1) recognize or name the feeling; (2) ask the questions; and (3) identify the bad, negative, or inaccurate thought.

Step 6: Discuss Handout 14, Common Styles of Thinking

To introduce handout 14 to the patient, you may use the following script:

Often the thoughts that lead to upsetting feelings are illogical in some way or related to some kind of thinking that doesn't make sense. There are certain types of thinking that are very common and almost always lead to distress. When you're able to identify when you're using these types of thinking, you'll be a lot better at being able to deal with negative feelings. Some people refer to these patterns as "stinking thinking." Let's review some of these.

Read handout 14 with the patient. Describe each style of thinking. Ask the patient to try to identify what style of thinking he or she used in the last example you mentioned or in other examples from his or her life.

Step 7: Discuss Handout 15, Cognitive Restructuring (CR): Steps 1, 2, and 3

To introduce handout 15 to the patient, you may use the following script:

Often people aren't aware of the thoughts that lead to their feelings in different situations. This is very common. Often people feel scared or sad in a certain situation, and they're not sure why. That's why one of the first steps of CR is to keep track of upsetting situations and the emotions and thoughts you have about those situations. This handout will help you do that. Let's use the situation we talked about earlier as an example, and I'll show you the steps. *This is only a five-step program!*

Today we'll only be working on the first three steps.

Be sure the patient has a copy of the handout. Point out the headings and names to the first three steps. If helpful, you can use the following script to walk the patient through the steps:

> In *step 1,* you write down the upsetting *situation.* Let's use the example we discussed earlier. So I'll write, "saw friend who didn't say hello."
>
> In *step 2,* you identify the upsetting *feeling* you experienced in this pretend situation or scenario. So I'll write "hurt" in the blank space. Sometimes a person feels more than one emotion in a situation. That's okay. Focus on the strongest or most upsetting feeling. There are some questions you can ask yourself to help identify your feelings.
>
> In *step 3,* you identify your *thoughts* about the situation. Remember, our thoughts lead to our feelings, so to deal with upsetting emotions, we need to understand more about what you're thinking in different situations. In this situation, you see a friend who doesn't say hello and you feel hurt. If this actually happened to you, what thoughts might go through your mind that could lead to hurt or sadness? We'll write those thoughts down here in step 3 under the heading "Thought."
>
> Now, often you might have more than one thought about a situation. When that happens, you choose the one thought that is the most upsetting or is most strongly related to your strongest feeling about the situation. Write it down in step 3.
>
> The second part of step 3 involves identifying the type or common style of the thinking. Remember handout 14, Common Styles of Thinking? Use it to help you. Now, what style or type of thought should be written down in step 3? For now, leave the last column blank.

Review handout 14 with the patient. Help the patient consider which style of thinking is most associated with the thought he or she listed. Convey that there is no "correct" answer regarding the style of thought selected. The therapeutic piece is for the patient to recognize that these styles often overlap, and that these styles can lead to different interpretations of situations. Understanding that styles are being used helps the patient to develop some flexibility in the kinds of thoughts he or she has about situations.

Step 8: Summarize Module 6 for the Patient

Summarize for the patient what he or she learned in this module. Since this material is critical to the success of CR skills, patients will need some extra help in understanding the process.

Remind patients that in this module, he or she learned

- to distinguish different feelings
- that in distressing situations, he or she can (1) name the feeling, (2) ask the questions, and (3) identify the thoughts that influence how he or she feels
- that one important way to deal with negative feelings is to work on the thoughts that lead to those feelings
- to use a three-step approach to resolve negative feelings by (1) identifying the situation, (2) identifying the feeling, and (3) identifying the thought and the style of negative thinking it might represent
- to practice CR until the next session

Step 9: Assign Practice/Homework

Since CR is believed to be the core ingredient of effective CBT for co-occurring disorders, the skills the patient will acquire in this module are crucial. Learning the skills in the session is just the first step. Homework and practice and more practice are essential to internalizing the skill and making the process increasingly automatic. Here are verbatim instructions you can follow to close the session introducing CR. You will need to have extra copies of handout 15, Cognitive Restructuring (CR): Steps 1, 2, and 3, available for the patient to complete the practice.

Give the patient numerous copies of handout 15 that he or she can use at home. When assigning homework, you may use the following script:

For homework, I'd like you to fill out several of these handouts for upsetting things that happen this week. Complete steps 1, 2, and 3, just like we did here today. First write down a few things about the situation, like what happened and who was involved. Then think about what you were thinking and feeling after the situation. Sometimes you may just be aware of having feelings and may not be sure what you were thinking about or what happened that made

you feel that way. That's okay. Use handout 13, Guide to Thoughts and Feelings, to help you figure out what you were thinking. Then try to figure out what happened that led to these thoughts and feelings. Also use handout 14, Common Styles of Thinking, to help you identify the style or type of thought in each situation.

Work through one or two handouts using recent situations in your life or anything you want. Use handouts 13 and 14. Think about the connection between your thoughts about the situation and your associated emotions.

Try to fill out one handout each day. Try to fill out these handouts as soon as possible after something happens or after you realize you're feeling something. This will make it easier for you to figure out your thoughts and feelings.

Ask the patient, "How many handouts can you commit to filling out before our next session?" Help the patient be realistic in setting the assignment. One handout is acceptable. Two would be excellent. Be sure the patient has extra handouts to complete the practice assignment.

Note the answer and remind the patient that you will follow up with him or her on the homework during the next session.

Encourage the patient to attend peer support group(s) between sessions.

Encourage the patient to practice breathing retraining twice a day before the next session. Emphasize that practicing the skill on a regular basis when he or she is not distressed (such as when getting up in the morning) will help develop and internalize the skill. Then he or she will be able to use it better in times when it's really needed.

Step 10: Write Your Clinical Observations

Ask yourself the following questions to help you evaluate the effectiveness of this module. It might be more insightful if you actually record the answers on a separate sheet of paper.

- Did the patient seem to be able to use the handouts?
- Which handouts seemed easier or more difficult for the patient to understand?
- Were you able to instill a sense of humor into the common styles of thinking segment?

Step 11: Review the Therapeutic Alliance

Since CR is the core ingredient of CBT, it will be critical to understand and explore the patient's experience in approaching and learning these skills. Try to model, focus on reinforcing small steps, affirm motivation, emphasize non-judgmental responses, and underscore the importance of practicing between sessions. This module may take one to two sessions in order for the patient to feel comfortable identifying feelings, making connections to thoughts, and then breaking down the first three steps of CR. Situations that patients bring in may or may not be related to their core psychiatric symptoms at this juncture. This is acceptable until they master the skill. In fact, approaching more highly charged emotional situations is often too difficult. The skills are often easier to learn at this stage by using mild to moderately intense everyday experiences.

Step 12: Complete the Clinician and Supervisor Checklists

In conclusion, review the Clinician Checklist (and, if appropriate, the Supervisor Checklist) found on the program CD-ROM, and record the appropriate information for each patient and/or group.

• • •

Duplicating this page is illegal. Do not copy this material without written permission from the publisher.

95

Cognitive Restructuring:
The Five-Step Program

Goals

- Demonstrate to the patient how thoughts determine or influence feelings.
- Define automatic thoughts and demonstrate how they can adversely affect feelings.
- Teach the patient the five-step program of CR.
- Help the patient connect distressing feelings to certain situations, identify the thoughts, and create a new thought or action plan.

Time

Since this material is the core ingredient of CBT for co-occurring disorders, this module may be repeated as often as necessary for the patient to achieve some degree of efficacy in doing CR. This typically may be two to four sessions.

- 45–50 minutes for an individual session
- 60–90 minutes for a group session

Handouts Needed

- Handout 16: *The Five-Step Program of Cognitive Restructuring (CR)*
- Handout 17 (optional): *My Most Distressing Feelings*
- Handout 20 (optional): *Payoff Matrix*

For thumbnail views of these handouts, see pages 119 and 120.

▼

Suggested Session Outline

Step 1: Review Practice/Homework

Review the patient's work on handouts 13, 14, and 15 from the previous session. Remind the patient how many of handout 15 he or she committed to completing (steps 1–3). Review the patient's work. It is critical that patients become competent in working these first three steps before progressing to the remaining steps in this session.

Ask if the patient attended other planned treatment and peer support group(s) between sessions. Discuss this if appropriate.

Step 2: Introduce CR and Review Homework

In introducing this session and the idea of homework review, you may use the following script:

> **Today, we're going to continue to work on cognitive restructuring, or CR. This time we are going to cover *all five steps*. Last time we met, we talked about only three steps. We also talked about how what you think is connected to what you feel. Let's review your homework before we talk more about thoughts and feelings.**

Review the handouts and reinforce compliance. Highlight the connection between thoughts and emotions. At this stage of CR, do not challenge distorted thinking. If the patient had difficulty with the homework or did not complete the homework, complete handout 15, Cognitive Restructuring (CR): Steps 1, 2, and 3, in the session with the patient for at least one situation from the previous week. Role-model the use of handout 13, Guide to Thoughts and Feelings, while completing handout 15. Again, highlight for the patient how different thoughts lead to different feelings. Reinforce the patient's ability to identify a situation and his or her thoughts and feelings in that situation.

Often patients confuse thoughts and feelings. For example, you may find a patient writes thoughts in both the thoughts and feelings columns of handout 15. When this happens, refer to handout 13, Guide to Thoughts and Feelings, and label the four basic emotions. Ask the patient which of the four feelings best fits the statement in the "Thought" column. Then point out to the patient that what was listed in the "Feeling" column was actually another thought that could be listed in the "Thought" column. Tell him or her that the Feeling column should be reserved for one (or more) of the four basic feelings. Encourage your patient to use the words "I think that . . ." when describing thoughts and "I feel . . . " when describing feelings.

If the patient completed homework and brought in numerous examples, select one from handout 15. Conduct an analysis of one particular situation. Only this time, ask the patient to list a new or alternative thought. For example, you may use the following script:

> **Okay, so let's look more closely at one of the situations you wrote about. Remember, we talked about the fact that the way we think, or the things we think, influences how we feel. So let's look at this situation you wrote about.**

> **In this situation, you thought _____ (restate patient's thought) and that made you feel _____ (restate patient's emotion). What would you have felt if you thought _____ (propose alternative thought that would lead to another feeling)? (Pause for the patient's response.) Yes, good. If you had thought _____ (alternative thought) instead of _____ (original thought), you would have felt _____ (new feeling) instead of _____ (old feeling).**

Step 3: Illustrate to Patient How Life Experience Shapes Thinking

Demonstrate to the patient how life experience shapes thinking. You might say:

> **So given any situation that you experience, you might experience different emotions depending on what you think about that situation. Correct?**

Pause and be sure the patient is in agreement.

> **So what makes people think the things they do? Well, mostly life experiences shape people's thinking. Over the course of your lifetime, you've learned certain ways of understanding or thinking about things from all your different experiences, including ones associated with your mental health problems. So if you suffer from depression, you may be inclined toward pessimistic or negative thoughts; if you have anxiety, you may be inclined to thoughts that**

see people or situations as threatening; or if you have trauma in your background, you may believe that the same thing will happen to you again and again . Do you see that?

Seek the patient's agreement. If the patient doesn't agree, explore his or her reasoning.

Step 4: Illustrate "Automatic Thoughts" to the Patient

Demonstrate to the patient how ingrained and automatic thinking can be. You might say:

Over time, those negative ways of thinking about yourself or other people or the world become ingrained and automatic. They can become so automatic that you aren't even aware of them. But even if you aren't aware of these automatic thoughts and beliefs, they still affect how you feel in the situations you experience.

These automatic thoughts aren't always true or helpful, although most of us just take for granted that they are true. But just because someone thinks something, it doesn't mean it's true. So most of us have these automatic thoughts that we picked up through our life experience. These automatic thoughts aren't always true or helpful. Even so, we still believe them, and these beliefs can make us feel lousy.

Step 5: Demonstrate to the Patient How to Challenge One's Thoughts

Demonstrate to the patient how automatic thinking can influence us negatively, but these thoughts can be challenged and altered for the better. You might say:

Okay, so what do we do about these unhelpful thoughts (or beliefs) that can make you feel really lousy?

Well, first we learn about what you think in different situations. You've already started doing this by filling out handout 15 on CR. The next step involves evaluating your thinking to see if it makes sense or is helpful to you. Remember, you think lots of things that you accept as true in part because that's just how you've thought for so long. We want to really look at that and evaluate whether what you think in different situations makes sense. If we decide that your thoughts in a particular situation aren't helpful, we can

change them. Usually, if you change unhelpful thoughts, you feel better!

There are several questions you can ask yourself that will help you look at your thoughts more objectively. The first question to ask yourself is "What evidence do I have for this thought?"

Other questions you can ask yourself are

• Is there a different way of looking at the situation?

• Is there a different possible explanation?

• How would someone else think about the situation?

• Are my judgments based on how I felt rather than what I did?

Asking yourself these questions about the situation you are working on will help you evaluate whether your thinking is balanced and helpful. Any questions? Okay, let's work through an example together.

This time we are doing all five steps!

Step 6: Discuss Handout 16, The Five-Step Program of Cognitive Restructuring (CR)

Make numerous copies of handout 16 for the patient. Tell the patient you want to work through a recent simple situation that was distressing for the patient to demonstrate the process of challenging a thought. Enlist the patient's active participation.

Have the patient identify a recent distressing situation. Have him or her record the situation in the blank space on the handout. Use a simple situation to demonstrate the process of evaluating a thought and then taking action. Remember to focus on only one situation, feeling, and thought or belief, though many may be at first associated with the situation.

Next, have the patient circle the feeling or feelings most strongly associated with the situation.

Help the patient identify the thought most strongly related to the feeling above and record it on the handout. Then ask the patient to circle the common style of thinking used in the example. Ask the patient to decide if this thought "makes sense" or is helpful to him or her. Take time here to emphasize which of these common styles best characterizes the patient. Can he or she identify which style most frequently characterizes his or her thinking?

Ask the patient to list evidence for and against the truth of his or her thought recorded in step 3 of the handout. Then ask the patient to "weigh" the evidence and decide if it supports or doesn't support his or her thinking. Have the patient check whether the thought is or is not supported by the evidence.

Finally, in the last step of the handout, encourage your patient to take action either through developing a new thought that is supported by the evidence and/or developing a plan of action for dealing with a situation. Restate that this illustrates the process of challenging his or her thinking.

You may use the following script:

The last step of CR involves taking action. Once you've weighed the evidence, it's time to decide if the evidence supports your thoughts or if it doesn't support your thoughts. Consider all the available evidence and decide if your thought or belief is accurate or not. Ask yourself if you could convince another person that your belief was true. If the evidence doesn't support your thinking, then it's time to develop a new, more accurate or balanced thought to replace the old thought. This new thought should be supported by the evidence you have.

If the evidence supports your thinking, then it's time to develop a plan for dealing with the upsetting situation. Think about whether you need more information about the situation, what steps you need to take to improve the situation, if the situation poses serious safety issues, or if you can enlist someone's help in dealing with the problem.

Any questions about what we've talked about today? Let's spend some time working through all the steps with another situation.

Step 7: Summarize Module 7 for the Patient

Summarize for the patient what he or she learned in this module. Since this material is critical to the success of CR skills, patients will need some extra help in understanding the process.

Remind patients that in this module, he or she learned

- to weigh the evidence supporting or not supporting his or her thoughts
- to further discuss common styles of thinking that often lead to distress
- to take action either through developing a new thought or a plan of action

Step 8: Assign Practice/Homework

Since CR is believed to be the core ingredient of effective CBT for co-occurring disorders, the skills the patient will acquire in this module are crucial. Learning the skills in the session is just the first step. Homework and practice and more practice are essential to internalizing the skill and making the process increasingly reflexive. Here are verbatim instructions you can follow to close this second session about CR. Be sure you have copies of handout 16, The Five-Step Program of Cognitive Restructuring (CR), to give to the patient to complete the practice assignment.

To explain the homework to the patient, you may use the following script:

For homework, I'd like you to fill out handout 16, The Five-Step Program of Cognitive Restructuring (CR), for situations you experience. This week I'd like you to fill out *all five steps*. List the evidence you have that supports your thinking, then list the evidence you have that doesn't support your thinking. Remember, evidence needs to be something concrete or specific. Also use handout 13, Guide to Thoughts and Feelings, when you need help figuring out your thoughts and feelings in a particular situation. Once you've considered all the evidence for your thought, decide if the evidence supports your thinking or not. If it doesn't, write a new thought that is supported by the evidence. If the evidence does support your thinking, decide what you can do to deal with the upsetting situation. I'd also like you to read handout 14, Common Styles of Thinking, and to figure out which styles of thinking come up for you in the situations you write about this week.

How many of the five-step handouts can you commit to completing between now and our next session?

Help the patient be realistic in setting the assignment. One handout is acceptable. Two would be excellent. Be sure the patient has extra handouts to complete the practice assignment. Remind the patient that this work is difficult for most people and not to get discouraged if it feels hard. Ask the patient to do the best he or she can during the rest of your meetings together.

Encourage the patient to attend planned treatment and peer support group(s) between sessions.

Encourage the patient to practice breathing retraining twice a day before the next session. Emphasize that practicing the skill on a regular basis when he or she is not distressed (such as when getting up in the morning) will help develop and internalize the skill. Then he or she will be able to use it better in times when it's really needed.

Step 9: Write Your Clinical Observations

Ask yourself the following questions to help you evaluate the effectiveness of this module. It might be more insightful if you actually record the answers on a separate sheet of paper.

- Did the patient seem to be able to use the handouts?

- Which handouts seemed easier or more difficult for the patient to understand?

- Was the patient able to be flexible in evaluating the evidence? In changing the thought? In being able to reflect on his or her interpretation of events?

Step 10 (Optional): Discuss Handout 17, My Most Distressing Feelings

As you complete your second session of CR, it may be useful to start a third session by administering a generic or specific screening measure checklist (see the curriculum *Screening and Assessment*). These may include the Modified Mini Screen (MMS), the Center for Epidemiologic Studies Depression Scale (CES-D Scale), the Social Interaction Anxiety Scale (SIAS), or the PTSD Checklist (PCL). These measures may serve to focus the CR on the symptoms that could still be most troublesome to the patient. Once the patient completes a screening measure in your presence, it will be useful to go over his or her responses. Doing CR with those responses still indicative of problems would be important at this juncture.

Handout 17 may be worth distributing at this point. This handout encourages the patient to increase the degree of difficulty by using CR on more distressing symptoms.

Use handout 17 only if you are comfortable with the patient's progress in mastering the CR techniques, and you have assessed the patient's own stability and comfort in approaching potentially more challenging emotional material. This may be especially helpful for patients with PTSD who may need to approach re-experiencing or avoidance symptoms, or for patients with thought disorders who may need to approach delusional beliefs.

Step 11: Review the Therapeutic Alliance

Forging a working alliance with the patient through the five-step CR process is likely critical to the effectiveness of the CBT. At this juncture, many patients have developed some competence in the first three steps. This is to be affirmed and supported. Often the challenge for patients is developing flexibility to interpret the evidence. Two familiar techniques are often used to help a patient do this. One is the "reality TV show." What if audience members were watching a situation that the patient experiences? What would they likely conclude from observing the situation? Would all of the audience agree or would they have a difference of opinion? How many different opinions might there be? Some patients might even use percentages to describe the various probabilities. Another approach is the "courtroom." The patient considers the evidence and thinks about what a jury would decide. The key is that the patient moves away from a fixed and rigid interpretation of events and situations.

At this juncture, the cognitive-behavioral change comes in repetition of the skill. It is, of course, important to ensure that the patient is working through the five steps in a correct manner, but it is with the repetition of these steps that the process becomes increasingly internalized.

Homework remains important. If homework is not turned in, then the sessions consist of generating a situation over the past week and then running through the five-step process. Do as many of these as can be processed within the duration of the session.

Also, at this juncture, it will be important to begin to process core psychiatric disorder symptoms and their associated effects. Some patients who are obviously symptomatic will be very willing to approach these situations. Other patients will focus on more current daily life-stress situations in their homework. For these patients, it is recommended that you acknowledge the importance of these current stressors in an empathic way and then transition to issues related to the psychiatric disorder. You are wise not to give in to the patient's efforts to entirely avoid the discussion of his or her primary psychiatric disorder symptoms, including PTSD material. Anxiety disorders associated with avoidance strategies (social anxiety, agoraphobia, and panic disorder) may also need a more intentional focus on the part of the clinician for inclusion in CR examples. Handout 20, Payoff Matrix, is specifically included to be certain PTSD "feelings" can be addressed. It can also be used to examine other thoughts.

Since this is the "working through" stage of CBT, in individual formats it is possible that two to four or even five sessions could be dedicated to CR. In group formats, however, the number of sessions dedicated to CR could be predetermined. During this stage the patient may be making noticeable changes. These improvements should be verbalized and affirmed. Also, it is important to bring in the patient's list of goals and examine if he or she is any closer to these goals or at least envisioning them more positively.

Refer to chapter 6 of this guide for suggestions on how to approach special issues for patients with co-occurring disorders, specifically in acquiring the CR skill set.

Step 12: Complete the Clinician and Supervisor Checklists

In conclusion, review the Clinician Checklist (and, if appropriate, the Supervisor Checklist) found on the program CD-ROM, and record the appropriate information for each patient and/or group.

• • •

MODULE 8

Generalization and Beyond

Goals

- Review the entire seven previous modules and their goals with the patient.
- Review the three basic skills first identified in module 1.
- Review the three goals first identified in handout 5 and the Fact Sheet on the patient's specific disorder.
- Terminate CBT for co-occurring disorders and make a referral if appropriate.

Time

This module may take more than one session to complete.

- 45–50 minutes for an individual session
- 60–90 minutes for a group session

Handouts Needed

- Handout 18: *Summing Up*
- Handout 19: *Serenity*
- Handout 5: *Goals: Positive Psychology* (for review only)

  For thumbnail views of these handouts, see pages 116 and 119.

- Fact Sheet on the patient's specific disorder (for review only)

▼

Suggested Session Outline

Step 1: Review Practice/Homework

Ask the patient if he or she continued to practice the breathing retraining exercise twice a day as instructed. If not, encourage the patient to practice this technique two or three times a week. Explore any issues the patient may have encountered that prevented him or her from practicing. If the patient did practice, explore the benefits of practice.

Review the patient's work on handout 16 and, if assigned, handout 17 from the previous session. Remind the patient how many of handout 16 he or she committed to completing (steps 1–5). Review the patient's work. It is critical that patients become competent in working all five steps of CR.

Ask if the patient attended planned treatment and peer support group(s) between sessions. Discuss this if appropriate.

Step 2: Introduce the Final Module and Session

To begin summarizing and reviewing what the patient or group has learned, you may use the following script:

> **We have spent the last few months working together to help you learn about, understand, and manage negative emotions related to your experiences with a co-occurring psychiatric and substance use disorder. You've worked really hard and have done well. You've made a lot of progress over this time, and I'd like to talk about your progress and also talk about ways for you to continue to use the skills you learned in therapy after we stop meeting. I'd also like to use the time in this session to summarize a few points and complete two handouts.**

> **Some patients feel a little anxious at the prospect of ending treatment and wonder if they will be able to manage on their own. Let's talk about that for a moment. The major focus of this treatment program has been on helping you develop the skills necessary to cope with negative emotions and distress, and to cope with these kinds of difficult feelings without using drugs and alcohol. These**

skills can help you get on with your life and pursue goals that are important to you.

Ask the patient the following questions:

- **How are you feeling about your progress?**
- **How are you feeling now compared to when you began the program?**
- **How are you feeling about your ability to manage the things we've been talking about without using drugs and alcohol?**

Allow the patient (or group) time to reply to these questions.

Step 3: Review Handout 18, Summing Up

Mention the three basic skills of CBT listed at the beginning of handout 18. Review the first four questions with the patient, and have him or her either record the replies verbally or in writing on the handout.

Review the basic three skills first identified in module 1. The three skills that the patient learned were (1) breathing retraining, (2) identifying primary symptoms and other issues of the co-occurring psychiatric disorder, and, finally, (3) cognitive restructuring.

In reviewing the three skills, you may use the following script:

Let's review some of the skills you've been learning during our sessions. First, we spent some time early in treatment to learn an important skill for dealing with anxiety and physical tension— breathing retraining. Over the course of treatment, I've been pleased to hear about how you practiced this skill and your ability to use it in a variety of situations where you felt anxious. (Give an example, if appropriate.)

- **How has breathing retraining been helpful? In what situations did you find it helpful?**

Allow the patient time to share verbally and/or to record his or her answers on the handout.

Second, we spent some time learning about your psychiatric disorder and how it relates to your use of substances and feelings. (Personalize this script to address the patient's specific emotional difficulties.) You also learned about having co-occurring disorders

and that many people with co-occurring disorders have shared the same struggles and hopes as you.

- **In what ways did you find learning about the symptoms of co-occurring disorders helpful?**

Allow the patient time to share verbally and/or to record his or her answer on the handout.

Finally, the third skill you have learned is cognitive restructuring, or CR. This skill has helped you see that unpleasant feelings are related to negative thoughts. By identifying the negative thoughts associated with unpleasant feelings and evaluating the evidence supporting those thoughts, you have learned that you can change your thinking, and that these changes can improve your mood. As we've worked together, I've been really impressed with the progress you've made in CR, including your ability to identify negative thoughts and to challenge your own thinking.

- **What stands out for you as having been the most helpful part of cognitive restructuring?**

Allow the patient time to share verbally and/or to record his or her answer on the handout.

I think you have done a great job of learning these three skills in CBT. However, like any other skill, such as bowling or tennis, you get better and better with more practice over time. We have found that many patients actually continue to improve after these CBT sessions are over. For this reason, it is important for you to keep practicing the skills that you've learned in therapy so that you get even better than you are now.

Ask the patient the following questions:

- **What were the most helpful things that we did?**
- **What skills have you found most helpful?**
- **What things were not very helpful?**
- **What skills do you think you need to continue to practice?**
- **What problems might you still be concerned about?**

Step 4: Review Handout 5, Goals: Positive Psychology

This is a good opportunity to refer back to handout 5. In this handout, the patient listed goals, or three things that would be possible to do if he or she were symptom free. Help the patient review and remember what he or she wanted out of life without the psychiatric symptoms. At this juncture, you and the patient can assess where the patient is relative to achieving these goals. Sometimes, patients will be able to reflect very positively on this benchmark check. Other times, they will notice that they fell short. You can typically point to progress made even if goals were not achieved. This segment of CBT must be done in a compassionate, nondefensive, and realistic way. That being said, you can also point to research with CBT that suggests that patients often continue to improve even after the therapy ends. Cover the following content with the patient in your own words or use the following script:

> **Another reason why patients often continue to improve after treatment is that they begin to rely more on their own skills rather than depending on their clinician. As patients look more within themselves for answers and skills for dealing with trauma-related experiences, and less to other people such as clinicians, their self-confidence increases, as well as their ability to get on with their lives.**
>
> **Let's talk about some situations in which you could use some of the skills that you've learned. For example, let's say that you suddenly felt short of breath and started to feel anxious. You could use your breathing retraining exercises to cope with your anxious feelings and to decrease your physiological arousal. Let's come up with a few more examples of situations in which you could use the other skills you've learned. How about cognitive restructuring? (Probe the patient and supply hints as necessary.)**

After discussing a few examples, you can say:

> **I strongly encourage you to continue practicing the skills you have learned. This will give you an important opportunity to improve your skills even more. I understand that it is possible that despite your efforts to practice and use the skills you have learned, you could still experience some distress and feel a need for additional treatment. If this occurs, there are a number of steps you can follow.**

Step 5: Review Handout 19, Serenity

Use this handout to encourage the patient to reflect on himself or herself and the changes made over the sessions. Ask the patient to discuss the things he or she cannot change, the things that can be changed, and how to know the difference between the things that can or cannot change. Ask the patient how he or she will identify when acceptance and courage are needed.

Step 6: Review the Fact Sheet on the Patient's Specific Disorder

At this point it may again be useful to refer to the Fact Sheet on your patient's specific disorder. Refer specifically to two sections: "How Does _____ Affect Addiction Treatment and Recovery?" and "Treatment for Co-occurring _____ and a Substance Use Disorder."

Review this Fact Sheet with the patient. Help the patient compare his or her own plan with what is generally recommended in the Fact Sheet.

Step 7: State These Preliminary Remarks before Concluding Treatment

If no follow-up appointments are scheduled, you may say:

> **I appreciate your participation in CBT for your co-occurring disorders. I hope you will continue to practice the skills that you have learned. As it stands, we have no further scheduled sessions. You are ready to use these skills in your life, on your own.**

Discuss the need for continuing in other treatment, referrals to new treatment, and attendance and participation at peer support group meetings (such as Alcoholics Anonymous, Narcotics Anonymous, or Dual Recovery Anonymous) in the community. Encourage the patient to practice breathing retraining. Also, if contact with or monitoring by you is an option, the plan and mechanics of doing this should be described.

Step 8: Conclude the Treatment

When you end treatment, include positive feedback and encouragement. If appropriate, emphasize that many patients do not experience the full benefits of treatment right away. Explain that continued improvement may be evident in the months to come as the patient continues to practice the skills he or she learned in therapy. The patient may need to be reminded of the importance of continuing in his or her addiction and mental health recovery program and peer support group meetings.

Ending CBT or any helping relationship can be a difficult process. If during the termination process, the participant experiences a slip, relapse, or psychiatric symptoms severe enough to significantly interfere with his or her functioning, you and the patient should consider how these symptoms may be related to termination. Explore means by which the patient can apply learning from this treatment, with the help of natural social support systems, to autonomously proceed toward resolving distress. If there is any doubt about your patient's ability to do so at the time of termination, a plan is made to recontact the patient by phone at a scheduled time (e.g., one week later) or sooner if the patient is in crisis to briefly discuss his or her status.

If a patient may be dangerous to self or others, or is at imminent risk of relapse to substance use, your priority is patient safety. Follow up as appropriate to ensure patient safety. Carefully and thoroughly document events. If an immediate intervention isn't needed, then direct the patient to follow his or her substance relapse and crisis prevention plan and contact the patient's primary counselor. Lastly, it may be necessary for the patient to continue in psychological or psychiatric counseling to continue to support the gains he or she has made. Many patients will have already been in therapy, so this will be a natural transition. For other patients, referral to ongoing therapy, in addition to addiction treatment, may be necessary.

Step 9: Complete the Clinician and Supervisor Checklists

In conclusion, review the Clinician Checklist (and, if appropriate, the Supervisor Checklist) found on the program CD-ROM, and record the appropriate information for each patient and/or group.

• • •

COGNITIVE-BEHAVIORAL THERAPY HANDOUTS
(THUMBNAIL VIEWS)

Handout 1

▼
Introduction to CBT

  1

What Is CBT?

"CBT" stands for cognitive-behavioral therapy. The CBT you will be receiving has three key parts: breathing retraining, education, and cognitive restructuring. These components are each effective in reducing symptoms such as anxiety, negativity, distress, irritability, and physical tension. Each of these ingredients is briefly described below.

- **Breathing retraining:** Breathing retraining involves learning a skill for achieving a relaxed state. Over time and with practice, you will learn how to use breathing retraining to relax in stressful situations and to reduce anxiety. By the end of these CBT sessions, through the use of breathing retraining, you will have developed an improved sense of control over your anxiety and distress.

- **Education:** Your clinician will teach you about co-occurring psychiatric and substance use disorders. You will learn about the primary symptoms of the psychiatric disorder, the causes, and how it interacts with your use of drugs and alcohol. You will also learn about effective treatments to help you in your recovery. Knowing this information will help you deal with your problems in a more straightforward and effective way.

- **Cognitive restructuring:** Cognitive restructuring, or CR, involves learning to identify and then challenge the thoughts and beliefs that cause you distress. You will use self-monitoring to increase your awareness of thoughts that lead to distress. You will learn to identify patterns in your thinking that

Treatment for Your Alcohol or Drug and Mental Health Problems

This CBT is specifically designed for co-occurring substance use and mental health problems and does not replace the additional services you need for alcohol or other drugs that you receive in an addiction treatment program. It will also not replace the mental health services you may be receiving, including medication, to help you manage these symptoms.

To achieve the maximum possible benefits of CBT, you will need to be active in the treatments and recovery activities that have been recommended to you. Attendance at and participation in peer support groups is also associated with good outcomes.

Your clinician will check in with you at the beginning of each session to evaluate your involvement with treatment for substance use and your attendance at peer support groups.

Page 1 of 2

Handout 2

▼
Substance Relapse and Crisis Prevention Plan

2

(1) The early warning signs that I may be about to relapse to alcohol or drugs are

a. _____

b. _____

c. _____

Examples: going to places where I used drugs or drank alcohol; hanging out with people I used or drank with; having cravings; coping with negative feelings such as fear, anger, or sadness; having problems sleeping; isolating myself; needing to feel comfortable dealing with people

(2) Feelings I experience when I want to start using are

a. _____

b. _____

c. _____

Examples: anger, sadness, boredom, nervousness, guilt, shame, excitement, overwhelmed, self-confidence, fear of people, confusion, loneliness, resentment, despair, fatigue

(3) The plan to be implemented when these early warning signs or feelings appear:

a. _____

b. _____

c. _____

Examples: call my doctor, sponsor, counselor, or a person who supports my recovery; go to a peer support group meeting

Page 1 of 2

Handout 3

▼
Breathing Retraining

3

Our breathing affects the way we feel. For example, when you're upset, you may take a deep breath to calm down. Or when you're anxious, you may breathe in quick, shallow breaths. Very often, when people become frightened or upset, they feel like they need more air and may hyperventilate. Sometimes when you are struggling with wanting to use alcohol or drugs, your breathing will also be accelerated. Taking a deep breath or breathing quickly often does not help. In fact, these often cause anxious feelings. Unless you are preparing for a really dangerous situation, you often don't need as much air as you take in. When you hyperventilate and take in more air, you signal your body to prepare for danger. If you feel anxious and want to calm down, you need to slow down your breathing and take in *less* air.

> You should take a normal breath and
> **exhale slowly**.
>
> It is **exhaling** that aids relaxation, not inhaling.

Breathing fast and taking deep breaths are common responses to stress and anxiety. Such habits can be hard to break. Learning to control your breathing takes daily practice. You will find it helpful to first practice during times when you are not anxious. Later, when you have learned breathing awareness and control, you will find it helpful in more stressful situations.

Some points to remember about breathing

▼ Increase your awareness of your breathing patterns.

▼ Slow down your breathing.

1...2...3...4

▼ Practice using these breathing retraining exercises to decrease your anxiety.

These tips will help you deal with relapse triggers and cravings to use alcohol or drugs.

Page 1 of 2

Handout 4a

▼
Primary Symptoms of Co-occurring Disorders

4a

The primary goal of patient education is to help you understand the nature of your psychiatric symptoms and how they intersect with your substance use. Although you will probably want to talk more about these symptoms and how they affect you, right now, the emphasis is on education about these disorders.

You will be asked to describe your experience with the symptoms of the disorder you have and discuss how each symptom applies (or doesn't apply) to you. Some you may identify with; others you may feel do not apply.

Try to connect these symptoms to your substance use. Discuss how your substance use works, how it helps you, how it hurts you, and, if possible, describe the sequence of events that caused you to use. This will help you with CR later.

Your CBT clinician has Fact Sheets for co-occurring disorders in general and for the most common mental health problems.

Specific Fact Sheets cover the following problems:

Anxiety and related disorders:	Mood disorders:	Thought disorders:
• Generalized Anxiety Disorder (GAD)	• Major Depression	• Schizophrenia
• Social Anxiety Disorder	• Persistent Depressive Disorder	• Schizoaffective Disorder
• PTSD	• Bipolar Disorder	
• Panic Disorder		
• Obsessive-Compulsive Disorder (OCD)		

After you receive a Fact Sheet(s), your clinician will

- review the description of the disorder with you
- review the causes of the disorder with you

Afterward, your clinician will complete handout 4B with you.

Page 1 of 1

COGNITIVE-BEHAVIORAL THERAPY HANDOUTS
(THUMBNAIL VIEWS)

Handout 4b

▼
Primary Symptoms of the Mental Health Problem

HANDOUT **4b**

Part I:
Reply to the following six questions.

1. List the primary symptoms of the mental health problem you have.

   a. _____

   b. _____

   c. _____

   d. _____

   e. _____

   f. _____

   g. _____

   h. _____

   i. _____

   j. _____

2. Circle the letter of the symptoms that you have experienced.

3. Place an "x" next to the symptoms that you are currently experiencing (or have experienced over the past month).

4. Which of these symptoms is the most disruptive or upsetting to you?

   _____

5. Which is the most frequent?

   _____

Page 1 of 2

Handout 5

▼
Goals: Positive Psychology

HANDOUT **5**

Many people seek treatment in order to eliminate the negative symptoms of their mental health problems from their lives; however, people are generally more motivated to change because of the positive things that will happen. Think about how your mental health symptoms have interfered with your life and made you unable to obtain the things you want for yourself. Examples of such things may be a job, relationships, ability to leave the house, sexual relations, or driving a car.

1. **Answer the questions below and fill in the appropriate boxes.**

What are your three worst symptoms?	What are the major ways these symptoms interfere with your life?	What would you like to do if these symptoms were out of your way?
1		
2		
3		

2. **What are the top three things or goals you could do/achieve if you were symptom free?**

   a. _____

   b. _____

   c. _____

Page 1 of 1

Handout 6

▼
Difficulties Associated with Co-occurring Disorders

HANDOUT **6**

Many people with co-occurring disorders also experience other symptoms or problems that interfere with their lives and cause them distress. This handout will describe some of the difficulties associated with co-occurring disorders.

- First, people with mental health problems often use alcohol or drugs to cope.

- Second, people commonly experience difficulty with four types of negative feelings: fear and anxiety, sadness and depression, guilt and shame, and anger.

- Third, people who have co-occurring disorders often have difficulty in their relationships with other people.

The purpose of the next section of handouts is to help you recognize some of the difficulties associated with co-occurring disorders that you might experience. Many people find it helpful to understand that the distressing symptoms they experience are common and even "normal" for a person with co-occurring disorders. *You are not alone!* Many of these symptoms helped you survive, but their continued presence in your life is distressing and interferes with your daily activities. The first step in learning to manage these symptoms is to understand how and why they occur.

For this session or sessions, the handouts will cover:

Negative Feelings
- Fear and Anxiety (handout 8)
- Sadness and Depression (handout 9)
- Guilt and Shame (handout 10)
- Anger (handout 11)

Relationship Difficulties
(handout 12)

Drug and Alcohol Problems
(handout 7)

Page 1 of 1

Handout 7

▼
Drug and Alcohol Problems

HANDOUT **7**

Most patients with mental health issues also have problems with drugs or alcohol. They may try to avoid negative symptoms or feelings by using drugs or drinking. They may use substances to try to take away strong negative feelings such as anxiety, sadness, guilt, or anger; however, drugs and alcohol probably make some of these feelings worse over time.

In addition, patients who have psychiatric disorders often have sleep problems, such as trouble falling asleep or nightmares and may use drugs or alcohol to try to sleep better. Although using drugs and alcohol for this purpose might seem helpful at first, drugs and alcohol interfere with your body's ability to sleep well. Patients who use a lot of drugs or alcohol can end up with more sleep problems.

So, even though patients may use drugs or alcohol to try to feel better, this strategy can have a boomerang effect and make things worse. Trying to stop drinking or using drugs can be very scary, especially if you, and maybe many of your close friends and family, have been doing it a long time. Your involvement in a treatment program and in Twelve Step or other peer support group will help you to reduce your reliance on drugs and alcohol for coping. Your participation in these CBT activities will also help.

Page 1 of 2

Handout 8

▼
Fear and Anxiety

The feelings of anxiety and fear that you may experience are associated with most psychiatric disorders. Usually the fear and anxiety are irrational or disproportionate to a threat.

You may have fears of physical harm or abuse, being rejected or abandoned, or even being embarrassed or humiliated. You may also be afraid of becoming anxious or feeling unsettled. Physiologically, fear and anxiety can be understood as reactions to a dangerous and life-threatening situation. You may experience arousal in your body, intense emotional reactions, or fearful thoughts. You may view the world as an unsafe place and have concerns about your personal safety. Some common strategies to alleviate the anxiety and distress are to try to avoid places, people, or things that trigger your fears, and to try to distract yourself from your fearful thoughts.

(1) **In the space below, write down what triggers evoke your fear.**

Places:
_____
_____

People:
_____
_____

Activities:
_____
_____

Sounds, smells, sensations:
_____
_____

Page 1 of 2

Handout 9

▼
Sadness and Depression

**Common Emotions/
Loss of Interest**

Common emotions among those with co-occurring disorders are sadness and a sense of feeling down or depressed. You may have feelings of hopelessness and despair, frequent crying spells, and sometimes even thoughts of hurting yourself or suicide.

A loss of interest in the people and activities that you once found pleasurable is not uncommon. Nothing may seem fun to you. You may also feel that life isn't worth living and be disinterested in planning for your future.

Problems with self-image and a lack of self-confidence are also typical. You may tell yourself, "I am a bad person and bad things happen to me," or "If I had not been so weak or stupid, this would not have happened to me," or "I should have been tougher." Such thoughts contribute to feelings of sadness and depression. Your CBT clinician will help you become aware of these and other negative thoughts you may have that affect your self-image.

Memories may also cause you to recall unpleasant experiences. One negative experience can provoke memories of other negative experiences. This is the normal way in which your memory works. For this reason, you may find that memories of negative or even traumatic experiences may be accompanied by others that may be equally disturbing. These negative memories may be stirred up whenever you recall certain events. It may be difficult for you to think of other situations or experiences that are not so negative. This can increase your feelings of sadness and depression.

Please check all the responses that apply to you. ▼

My thoughts when I am sad or depressed are

☐ I am worthless.

☐ I don't have anyone I can depend on.

☐ Nothing will ever get better.

☐ My life is not worth living.

☐ Other: _____
_____

Page 1 of 1

Handout 10

▼
Guilt and Shame

Guilt and shame may be related to something you did or didn't do. It is common to second-guess your decisions or actions and blame yourself for what you did or thought you should have done.

People sometimes believe that having had bad experiences means they're bad people or somehow deserve the bad experiences.

You may experience feelings of guilt and shame.

Feeling guilty about what happened to you means that you are holding yourself responsible for things that may not have been preventable or were perhaps due to someone else's actions. These feelings of guilt can lead to helplessness, depression, and negative thoughts about yourself. Blame can also come from society, friends, family, and acquaintances because people often place responsibility on the person who has been hurt or victimized.

Some people may feel guilty or ashamed of having a mental health problem. Some feel that their emotional difficulties mean they are weak or bad. They feel that they have let their families or loved ones down, or that they are a failure. After having difficulties for a long time, people start to believe they are weak or bad, or that they should be able to deal with life better. These thoughts also lead to guilt and shame.

If you're feeling guilty or shameful, your CBT clinician will help you explore alternative ways to think about yourself, your life, and your mental health problem. Your clinician will help you develop strategies for confronting the people and situations you avoid because you feel guilty, ashamed, or unable to cope with shameful feelings.

Page 1 of 2

Handout 11

▼
Anger

Feelings of anger are common among people with co-occurring disorders. Your anger may be directed at a person (or persons) for causing you physical injury, for violating you, or for abusing you. It may be directed at people who treated you unfairly. You may see them as the cause of negative experiences in your life. You may be angry with people whom you trusted but who let you down. Other people, such as other motorists who cut you off when you are driving, may stir up your anger.

Many also find themselves angry and irritable toward those they love the most: family, friends, partners, and children. Sometimes you might lose your temper with people who are most dear to you. This may be confusing since you may not understand why you're so angry and irritable. While closeness with others may feel good, it also increases the opportunity for feelings of intimacy, dependency, vulnerability, and helplessness. Those feelings may make you feel angry and irritable because they remind you of how you may have felt during times in your life when you were close to people and bad things happened. In other words, you can get angry and irritable when you feel vulnerable to being hurt again.

You may find yourself so angry that you may want to lash out at someone in some way, or you actually may lash out. You may not recognize or know how to handle this anger. For some, this anger may never get expressed or come to the surface. It can feel scary or dangerous to express anger.

Page 1 of 2

COGNITIVE-BEHAVIORAL THERAPY HANDOUTS

(THUMBNAIL VIEWS)

Handout 12

HANDOUT 12

▼
Relationship Difficulties

It is not unusual for those with co-occurring disorders to have difficulty with relationships. Relationship problems may be a result of feeling sad, frightened, ashamed, or angry. These feelings can get in the way of feeling close to someone else.

If in your past you were rejected, humiliated, attacked, raped, or abused, it may be very difficult to trust people or to allow yourself to feel close to them. For many people, situations that involve intimacy and closeness with others stir up negative emotions. To cope with these negative feelings, you may withdraw or not participate in activities that involve others.

Sometimes people have sexual difficulties also. Feelings of sadness or depression may cause you to be less interested in sex. You might be less interested because sex may remind you of what happened in a prior relationship. Sometimes people avoid sex because it makes them feel vulnerable or anxious.

Sometimes the people you love the most and expect to be the most supportive are not. It is common for people

to experience anger, anguish, and guilt when people they love are hurt. You may find that your friends and family, especially your partner, may react negatively and have difficulty hearing about your addiction or psychiatric symptoms. They may not want to talk about them. They may want you to simply fix your alcohol, drug, or mental health problems because it makes them anxious. Getting support for what you are going through is very important. Because some people around you might find it difficult to talk about your experiences, they might not be able to provide the support you need. At the same time, the support of your family and friends plays an important role in your recovery. Talk to people whom you feel can support you and understand your feelings.

Page 1 of 2

Handout 13

HANDOUT 13

▼
Guide to Thoughts and Feelings

Feelings	Ask yourself	Related thoughts
Fear and anxiety	What bad thing do I expect to happen? What am I afraid is going to happen?	Thoughts that something bad will happen *Examples:* • Some terrible thing is going to happen. • I am going to be attacked or hurt. • I am going to be made fun of or humiliated. • I am going to be rejected or abandoned. • I am going to lose control or go crazy.
Sadness and depression	What have I lost? What is missing in me or in my life?	Thoughts of loss *Examples:* • I am worthless. • I don't have anyone I can depend on. • Nothing will ever get better. • Life is not worth living.
Guilt and shame	What bad thing have I done? What is wrong with me?	Thoughts of having done something wrong or being lacking in some way *Examples:* • I am inadequate. • I am to blame for things in my life. • I am a bad person. • I am a failure.
Anger	What is unfair about this situation? Who has wronged me?	Thoughts of being treated unfairly or having been wronged *Examples:* • I am being treated unfairly. • I am being disrespected. • I am being taken advantage of. • This situation is unfair. • Someone has done something wrong to me.

Page 1 of 1

Handout 14

HANDOUT 14

▼
Common Styles of Thinking

This handout is adapted from D. D. Burns, *The Feeling Good Handbook*, rev. ed. (New York: Plume, 1999).

All-or-nothing thinking	The world is seen in extremes or in "black and white" with no shades of gray. *Examples:* • "If you're not perfect, you're a failure." • "The world is either completely safe or totally dangerous."
Overgeneralization	You see a single distressing event as a never-ending pattern. When something bad happens, you automatically assume that it will happen again and again. *Examples:* • "Once a victim, always a victim." • "I was unable to keep myself safe before; therefore, I will always be unable to protect myself in the future."
"Must," "should," or "never" statements	These are unwritten rules or expectations for how you think you should behave that are based on myths, not facts. You may have learned these "rules" when you were growing up, and they may seem like they can never be changed. Yet they may make you feel uncomfortable, anxious, afraid, sad, or angry. *Examples:* • "I should be able to handle this." • "I never should have let it happen." • "I must stop thinking about my abusive experiences."
Catastrophizing	These thoughts occur when you focus on the most extreme and distressing possible outcome. Many times they are triggered by "what if" thoughts or result from a minor setback or unexpected problem. You then find yourself assuming the very worst will happen. *Examples:* • "What if I was in the bathroom and someone came in?" • "I didn't do well on this exam. I'm going to flunk the class." • You lose your temper, yell at your child, and then think, "He hates me and will never want anything to do with me ever again."

Page 1 of 2

Handout 15

HANDOUT 15

▼
Cognitive Restructuring (CR): Steps 1, 2, and 3

Fill out this chart as directed by your clinician.

Step 1: Situation	Step 2: Feeling	Step 3: Thought	Common style of thinking	New thought/ alternative thought

Please note: More than one common style of thinking may be related to the distressing feeling.

As we've discussed, people often have certain biased ways of thinking. These biases are very personal ways that people can overgeneralize, catastrophize, or engage in emotional reasoning.

(1) Do you tend to blame yourself or to be very critical of yourself? (Circle one) Yes No

If yes, which common style of thinking is this related to?

_____

(2) Do you tend to distrust other people? (Circle one) Yes No

If yes, which common style of thinking is this related to?

_____

Page 1 of 2

COGNITIVE-BEHAVIORAL THERAPY HANDOUTS
(THUMBNAIL VIEWS)

Handout 16

▼
The Five-Step Program of Cognitive Restructuring (CR)

 16

Step 1: Situation

Ask yourself, "What happened that made me upset?" Describe the situation.

_____

_____

_____

Step 2: Feeling

Circle your strongest feeling (if more than one applies, use a separate sheet of paper for each feeling):

Fear/Anxiety   Sadness/Depression   Guilt/Shame   Anger

Step 3: Thought

Ask yourself, "What am I thinking that is leading me to feel this way?" Use handout 13, Guide to Thoughts and Feelings, to identify the thought that is most strongly related to the circled feeling. Describe the thought below.

_____

_____

_____

If it applies, circle your common style of thinking:

All-or-nothing thinking	Emotional reasoning
Overgeneralization	Overestimation of risk
"Must," "should," or "never" statements	Inaccurate or excessive self-blame
Catastrophizing	Mental filter

Page 1 of 4

Handout 17

▼
My Most Distressing Feelings

 17

Distressing feeling	Connected to which mental health problem or situation in my life (past or present)	Underlying thought/ common style of thinking	New thought/ action plan

Page 1 of 1

Handout 18

▼
Summing Up

 18

Skills covered in the CBT sessions:

- Breathing retraining
- Education about co-occurring disorders
- Cognitive restructuring (CR)

① What things have gotten better since I started CBT?

  a. _____

  b. _____

  c. _____

② What things do I still want to work on after CBT ends?

  a. _____

  b. _____

  c. _____

③ Which skills from CBT will help me to work on these things?

  a. _____

  b. _____

  c. _____

④ What progress did I make on the three goals I listed in handout 5, Goals: Positive Psychology?

  a. _____

  b. _____

  c. _____

Page 1 of 2

Handout 19

▼
Serenity

19

Now that you've nearly finished the CBT sessions to help you with your co-occurring disorders and their effects on you, it's possible that you may have made some very important changes in how you view yourself and how you cope with the symptoms related to your disorders.

① What are the things about yourself and how you deal with situations and feelings that have changed? What things can you keep working at to change? Please explain.

  _____

  _____

  _____

  _____

② What are the things about yourself or how you deal with things that you have not changed, and maybe that you will be unable to change? Please explain.

  _____

  _____

  _____

  _____

Serenity Prayer

Recite the Serenity Prayer when you feel sad, frustrated, or disappointed about the things you cannot change. In peer support groups, particularly Twelve Step groups such as Alcoholics Anonymous, Narcotics Anonymous, and Dual Recovery Anonymous, people frequently recite the Serenity Prayer to help them manage times of distress. This action has been reported to be very helpful when encountering situations, thoughts, or feelings where you have no control. In other words, the Serenity Prayer helps when you are in a position of having to accept things the way they are and trust that everything will still be okay.

Serenity Prayer

God, grant me the serenity

To accept the things I cannot change,

The courage to change the things I can,

And the wisdom to know the difference.

Page 1 of 2

Handout 20

▼
Payoff Matrix

Please be as specific as possible about what you believe are the advantages and disadvantages of keeping your thought or belief (despite the evidence against it) versus changing the thought or belief to a more accurate one.

Advantages of *keeping* the thought or belief	Advantages of *changing* the thought or belief
In what ways does *holding on to* your thought or belief make your life seem more manageable, safer, or easier to handle? Does the thought or belief provide you with a sense of control, security, or predictability of the future?	How could *changing* your thought or belief improve your life? Consider whether changing your thought or belief would reduce distressing feelings and free you up from concerns about past events.

Disadvantages of *keeping* the thought or belief	Disadvantages of *changing* the thought or belief
In what ways does *holding on to* your thought or belief make life more difficult? Consider the role of the thought or belief in creating upsetting feelings for you and in restricting you from doing things you would like to do.	What are the possible disadvantages or costs of *changing* your thought or belief? Would changing the thought or belief cause you to feel less control, secure, or able to predict the future?

Page 1 of 1

Hazelden, a national nonprofit organization founded in 1949, helps people reclaim their lives from the disease of addiction. Built on decades of knowledge and experience, Hazelden offers a comprehensive approach to addiction that addresses the full range of patient, family, and professional needs, including treatment and continuing care for youth and adults, research, higher learning, public education and advocacy, and publishing.

A life of recovery is lived "one day at a time." Hazelden publications, both educational and inspirational, support and strengthen lifelong recovery. In 1954, Hazelden published *Twenty-Four Hours a Day,* the first daily meditation book for recovering alcoholics, and Hazelden continues to publish works to inspire and guide individuals in treatment and recovery, and their loved ones. Professionals who work to prevent and treat addiction also turn to Hazelden for evidence-based curricula, informational materials, and videos for use in schools, treatment programs, and correctional programs.

Through published works, Hazelden extends the reach of hope, encouragement, help, and support to individuals, families, and communities affected by addiction and related issues.

For questions about Hazelden publications,
please call **800-328-9000**
or visit us online at **hazelden.org/bookstore.**